T0323127

No
Snail

The story of L'Escargot,
the horse that foiled Red Rum

DAVID OWEN

fairfield books

First published by Fairfield Books in 2023

fairfield books

Fairfield Books
Bedser Stand
Kia Oval
London
SE11 5SS

© 2023 David Owen

ISBN 978-1-915237-21-7
Also available as an ebook: ISBN 978-1-915237-22-4

Every effort has been made to trace copyright and any oversight
will be rectified in future editions at the earliest opportunity.

The views and opinions expressed in this book are those of the author
and do not necessarily reflect the views of the publishers.

The moral right of David Owen to be identified as the author
of this work has been asserted in accordance with the
Copyright, Designs and Patents Act 1988.

A CIP catalogue record for is available from the British Library.

Typeset in Minion Pro by seagulls.net
Cover design by Steve Leard
Printed and bound by CPI Group (UK) Ltd, Croydon, CR0 4YY

This book is printed on paper certified by the Forest Stewardship Council

'For me, L'Escargot never properly received the credit he deserved.'

– Ginger McCain, trainer of Red Rum

Contents

Foreword vii

1   An extraordinary cargo 1
2   The Duchess's progeny 5
3   A peerless judge of horseflesh 9
4   Birth of an obsession 15
5   Myna birds and sonny boys 29
6   A refugee from Sussex 37
7   The beating of Garrynagree 42
8   Champion material 51
9   Yellow chrysanthemums and the surgeon's knife 61
10   Losing the Persian War 68
11   A whiff of Gatsby 77
12   It's a knock-out 82
13   A changing of the guard 90
14   A rival for the Grand National 98
15   Down in the mud 109
16   The new Leopardstown 115
17   Illustrious company 121
18   Going for the double 129
19   An instant dislike to Aintree 137

20 Duel 147

21 Best of the rest 157

22 Something different 166

23 The one to beat 173

24 A single-minded campaign 182

25 Avoiding the abyss, fulfilling the dream 188

26 One last grandstand finish 203

L'Escargot's racing record 210

Note on sources 215

Bibliography 217

Acknowledgements 220

Index 221

Foreword

Why L'Escargot? What persuaded me that it made sense to write at length about the 1975 Grand National winner almost half a century after the event?

There were many reasons. Firstly, I was surprised to discover that no book-length account of his career exists. The explanations for such lacunae are often persuasive. In L'Escargot's case, I have no doubt that it is a hole worth filling – in large part because he was so, so good. If you want one single fact to buttress this assertion, I would offer the following: before L'Escargot completed steeplechasing's 'double' of winning the Cheltenham Gold Cup (in 1970 and 1971) and the Grand National (in 1975), only one horse – Golden Miller – had previously done so. Since L'Escargot achieved the feat, not one of the forty-two Cheltenham Gold Cup winners has emulated him. Not one. And this in spite of the easing of the Aintree fences and the sharp increase in Grand National prize-money. L'Escargot and 'the Miller' – that is a pretty exclusive club.

Even so, as Donald 'Ginger' McCain, trainer of his great Grand National rival Red Rum, put it, L'Escargot 'never properly received the credit he deserved'. This is partly, I think, because the chestnut gelding's career came so soon after his incomparable compatriot Arkle's. While L'Escargot was active, many in and around racing were preoccupied, naturally enough, with trying to identify 'the next Arkle', just as footballers were once labelled 'the next Pelé', or cricketers 'the next Bradman'. No matter how good, no steeplechaser quite came up to scratch. Nearly half a century on, however, Arkle's shadow has finally begun to recede. I was pleased to see that my friend Robin Oakley's 2012 book, *Britain and Ireland's Top 100 Racehorses of All Time*, ranked L'Escargot at number twenty (seventh among steeplechasers). Yet, having studied his career in detail, I would be tempted to list him a place or two higher than that.

From his first race to his penultimate, it was uncanny how often the media of the day took more interest in his beaten opponent than in L'Escargot. This happened in the humble 'bumper' race at Navan with which he started his career: as Andrew Kavanagh, jockey of the beaten favourite, told me, 'On the day, it was the beating of Garrynagree, not the winning of L'Escargot.' It happened in his first Cheltenham Gold Cup, when all eyes were on the brilliant jumper Kinloch Brae, owned by Anne Duchess of Westminster. And it happened when – eventually – he won his Grand National: he was the party pooper preventing Red Rum from claiming an unprecedented hat-trick of Grand National victories. In a sense, even then, on that strange day at Aintree, L'Escargot couldn't win.

Nor did his retirement serve to cement his place in the esteem and affections of the Irish racing public, for whom he should by rights have been a bona fide hero, if not on Arkle's step of the podium then very close to it. An unfortunate misunderstanding resulted in him leaving the country where his exploits deserved to be most keenly fêted, to enjoy an opulent but secluded final decade 3,000 miles away in Virginia.

Part of the purpose of this book, then, is to illuminate L'Escargot's case for a more prominent place in horseracing's pantheon.

Another reason for writing it is L'Escargot's remarkable versatility. He won on the flat. He won over hurdles. And – the clincher – he won in the very different steeplechasing conditions of the USA. This transatlantic dimension means that L'Escargot's career weaves together the story of horseracing in three distinct countries – the USA, Britain and Ireland – in a unique way, and at a fascinating point in the sport's development. This web, indeed, extends to a fourth country, since L'Escargot's sire raced in France, being placed in both the Lyons and Vichy Derbys.

The early 1970s in Britain and Ireland was a time when money from corporate sponsorship gushed into racing, helping to inspire a burst of innovation. Even in the USA, where jump-racing was struggling to maintain a toehold in big urban centres, this period saw a hugely well-financed attempt to establish what might have become a world championship of steeplechasing. L'Escargot was in the thick of much of this activity, winning the inaugural Wills Premier Chase at Haydock Park in Lancashire, and running in the inaugural Colonial Cup – the fledgling world championship – at scenic Springdale in South Carolina.

My final justification for writing the book relates as much to the people closest to L'Escargot as to the horse himself. There are only a handful of basic story templates in sport. 'Underdog wins' is one; redemption narratives are another. L'Escargot's story is a powerful exemplar of a third story-type – that persistence pays off. By winning the Grand National at the fourth attempt, the horse clearly exemplified this. But the same is true, perhaps in even greater measure, of those around him. It was his jockey Tommy Carberry's first Grand National win at the eleventh attempt. His owner, Raymond Guest, a former US ambassador to Ireland, had won the Epsom Derby twice but he had not previously won a Grand National, in spite of becoming fascinated with the race all the way back in 1928 (an extraordinary renewal in which only two horses finished, and which also happened to be the first Grand National with commentary transmitted 'live' to the USA). L'Escargot's winning run was the thirteenth time a horse had carried Guest's famous chocolate-and-pale-blue colours in the Liverpool spectacular. L'Escargot's trainer Dan Moore had an even more poignant Grand National story: from his base, initially at Fairyhouse and then near The Curragh, he had been striving for thirty-seven years to make up for the deep disappointment of being beaten by a tiny margin when riding Royal Danieli to second place in Battleship's Grand National in 1938.

L'Escargot's 1975 Grand National victory was a hard slog for the horse, though he made it look comfortable. It was intensely cathartic for these three distinguished legends of the turf. This is their story as well as his.

The Milk Pail, December 2022

Chapter 1

An extraordinary cargo

A car-drawn horsebox turns into the tree-lined drive leading to an imposing farmhouse at Gilliamstown, 25 miles north of Dublin. There is nothing unusual about this: the 200-acre property hosts a well-known racing stable nestled beside a bright red barn. But, as it turns out, the horsebox carries an extraordinary cargo, and these are extraordinary times for the family that has lived and worked on the premises for around twenty years.

It is not possible, more than half a century later, to put an exact date on the delivery. The car-owner Thomas Matthews's best estimate is March or April 1965. This situates it within weeks of the crisp late-February morning when Jimmy Brogan, the Irish Grand National-winning trainer, fumbled for a cigarette at his favourite vantage point on the immaculate gallop adjoining the yard and collapsed, never to rise again. He was forty-six.

A placid, level-headed man with religious faith and a strong work ethic, Brogan had lived in the public eye for more than half his life. In 1938, while still a teenager, he had played a supporting role in one of the closest finishes in Grand National history. Looking the likely winner a couple of fences out – by which time Brogan had lost his cap, exposing his thick, dark hair to the newsreel cameras and the teeming Liverpool crowd – his mount, Workman, had ultimately tired on the long run-in, crossing the line in third place. Ahead of them, the American horse Battleship and Royal Danieli, another Irish challenger, fought all the way to the winning-post, separated albeit by the width of the course and the riderless Takvor Pacha. It was desperately close but, after they had flashed across the line, the diminutive Battleship – ridden by another teenager, Bruce Hobbs – was adjudged to have got up to win by a head. Royal Danieli's jockey, one Dan Moore, was to wait thirty-seven years before assuaging this Aintree disappointment.

Ten years later, by this time one of Ireland's top jockeys, Brogan came even closer to landing steeplechasing's biggest prize. Aboard a big, dark chaser called First Of The Dandies, he led all the way from the thirteenth fence, his mount's sheepskin noseband a constant and highly visible presence as the fortunes of others ebbed and flowed. It was not until the Elbow that a serious challenger, the mare Sheila's Cottage ridden by Arthur Thompson, loomed up on his inside. In a hard-fought duel over the famous race's agonising final stretch, the long-time leader clung on grimly but found himself losing ground with every stride. At the end of the two circuits, Sheila's Cottage had chiselled out a one-length winning margin. Carlow-born Thompson would triumph again four years later on Teal.

By then the unavoidable buffetings of the jump jockey's trade, including the vulnerabilities of a collarbone that had to be put back in place fourteen times and ended up being held together by wire, had helped to prompt a switch to training – and farming – for the master of Gilliamstown Cottage. He set about this with typical industry, meticulous attention to detail and a certain amount of guile. A row of a dozen or so red-doored stables was erected, with a Nissen hut positioned behind the farmhouse for the lads. The first box people would see when they drove in was reserved for the yard's latest winner. This was on the astute assumption that impressionable visitors were most likely to ask after the first head they saw poking over a stable door. As was not uncommon at the time, Brogan took to making up his own horse- and cattle-feed, exercising great care over both preparation and ingredients. Lads were instructed to plait the last couple of inches of the straw used for their charges' bedding, lest any unsightly wisps strayed outside to mess up the yard. 'My father hardly allowed birds to land on the gallop,' his daughter Pamela Morton remembers fondly.

Success duly arrived, notably in 1958, when horses trained by Brogan captured both the Irish Grand National and the coveted Galway Plate. His son Barry, who inherited every last scrap of Jimmy's riding ability and then some, states in a 1981 autobiography that his father could never decide which of these two exploits gave him more satisfaction. Crediting Jimmy with 'enormous patience and tact' as a trainer, Barry – who rode his first winner in May 1963, having only just turned sixteen – describes how, whenever a young rider was unable to cope with a difficult horse, Jimmy would 'hop up in his place' on the gallop or schooling yard and show him how it was done. He was, though, 'never a man to pat anyone on the back. You simply knew by his attitude whether he was pleased or disappointed.'

Barry also expresses admiration at the way his father 'worked non-stop to build up the yard and attract new owners'. One of the operation's most-valued owners was Major Bill Pilkington, a tall Englishman who came across regularly for the big meetings at Fairyhouse and Punchestown from his base at Shipton-under-Wychwood, on the edge of the Cotswolds. Clusium and Ballygowan, both repeated tenants of Gilliamstown's showcase first box, were Pilkington horses. It was the English major who Jimmy had in mind when thinking about a possible purchaser for the two-year-old chestnut gelding occupying Thomas Matthews's horsebox that day in 1965 when it turned into the Brogans' tree-lined drive.

Cattle were as much a part of the daily routine at Gilliamstown as racehorses. Barry recalls rising at four o'clock each morning to milk three cows and feed fifty calves. Jimmy also had a tract of land in Westmeath, some 40 miles away in the Irish midlands, which he used for wintering cattle and a few younger horses. This helped him to keep his finger on the pulse of this largely agricultural region. 'Cattle men were the kings of the country in those days,' according to Matthews.

It was there in the heart of Westmeath that Jimmy Brogan first set eyes on the long-legged yearling who would become L'Escargot.

Chapter 2

The Duchess's progeny

The acrid smell of coal smoke hangs in the air, catching the throat. Small, white-walled houses line the street. Modernity intrudes in the shape of a red-and-white For Sale sign on the wall of Lennon's, a 'Long Established' and 'High Profile' village shop. But for that and a sprinkling of the sort of cautionary Covid notices that had become wearily familiar by the winter of 2021, one might easily have imagined oneself transported back to 1977, the year Multyfarnham walked off with the National Tidy Towns title, outscoring 728 other communities. Passers-by too exude a courtesy that seems positively old-fashioned.

This is Ireland's damp, boggy heart. For all the country's silky-smooth new road network, it remains somewhat remote. Indeed, the site of Inny Junction, once known as the only railway station in the British Isles without a road to service it, is just a few miles up the line. Not far from the level-crossing on the road heading west out of the village is Rathganny. This is where the O'Neill family were based for some 200 years, in a fine double-fronted Georgian house with six bedrooms and a wall-hugging creeper trained across one corner.

Arthur O'Neill was a successful cattle man in the cattle country of Westmeath, founder and director of the Mullingar Livestock Agency. His wife Barbara, or Betty, had entered the thoroughbred trade in a small way after inheriting a single brood mare – Duchess Of Pedulas, or 'The Duchess' – from her mother. Little, seemingly, was expected of the mare, who had been foaled in 1929 and sold originally for just £18. Yet astonishingly, in 1950, she gave birth to a son, Mr What, who went on to win the 1958 Grand National, and by a handsome thirty lengths at that.

Interviewed after the race by the *Sunday Express*, Mrs O'Neill had professed to having wanted to breed a National winner 'all my life'. She described Mr What as 'a great pet', adding: 'We found it almost impossible to keep him in his stable. So we had to buy a padlock for his stable door.' She had not gone to Aintree to watch him because, she said, 'every time I have watched him he has lost'.

Cannily, Mrs O'Neill had kept one of The Duchess's female offspring, and in 1955 – the same year that she sold Mr What for £500 – this mare gave birth to a daughter named What A Daisy. Here too the O'Neills struck immediate pay dirt. What A Daisy's first foal, the colt Havago, won on debut at Dundalk in October 1963. The newcomer was sent off as the odds-on favourite in spite of the absence of prior form, indicating that the four-year-old's rich potential was already suspected.

By this time, two more What A Daisy foals had already been delivered in Rathganny's eight cut-stone stables. In both cases, the young mare had been mated with stallions based at Frank Latham's Blackrath Stud in County Kildare, just over 60 miles south-east of Multyfarnham. A rendezvous with the diminutive but fiery Vulgan, soon to emerge as one of the most successful stallions that jump-racing has known,[*] produced a filly, What A Honey. Then, in 1962, she returned to Blackrath's white-walled driveway, west of the Wicklow Mountains, for an assignation with the lesser-known and decidedly more even-tempered Escart III.[†]

Like Vulgan, Escart's roots were in France. Foaled the same year as What A Daisy, the colt compiled a solid if unspectacular flat-racing record around some of the country's provincial tracks. A busy three-year-old campaign saw him placed in both the Lyons and Vichy Derbys, before heading to Longchamp where he won the 1½-mile Prix de Madrid. He kept racing for two more years, obtaining a seventh and final victory in August 1960 in Vichy's Prix du Bourbonnais.

The Gallic origins of the two Blackrath stallions was no coincidence. When he bought Vulgan for £520 in the early 1950s, the quietly spoken Latham was acting on a theory or hunch. This was that the combination of a good, tough, French stayer and well-built Irish mares would produce successful racehorses, animals that would often be below average size but would come to maturity comparatively early. As he put

---

* Vulgan was the leading National Hunt sire on at least eleven occasions, including every year between 1966 and 1974. He sired three Grand National winners – Team Spirit (1964), Foinavon (1967) and Gay Trip (1970), as well as numerous other high-class hurdlers and steeplechasers, including Kinloch Brae, Larbawn, Salmon Spray and The Dikler.

† Escart would no doubt be better known if he had lived longer. The chestnut stallion died of a thrombosis in autumn 1966, aged just eleven. Other than L'Escargot, his best-known progeny included Doonbeg, Esban, Garoupe, General Symons, Lockyersleigh and Norwegian Flag.

it, sipping coffee in an interview with the *Irish Field* in the mid-1970s – by which time his conviction had been well and truly validated – the right stallion should 'pull together the big, rangey Irish mares and give them more quality'.

The near uniformly chestnut foal with the merest splash of white on his forehead who What A Daisy* produced as a consequence of her appointment with Escart – the future L'Escargot – would have been just a few months old when his half-brother Havago streaked to his maiden victory. It was probably a year or so after this that Jimmy Brogan, perhaps tipped off by another cattle dealer who lived close to his Gilliamstown base, paid Betty O'Neill a sum thought to have amounted to either £1,000 or £1,500 for the yearling.

That winter, Havago embarked on a brilliant four-race winning streak. The run culminated with victory in one division of the 1965 Gloucestershire Hurdle at Cheltenham. That streak would have filled Brogan with anticipation about what the horse's younger half-brother, still growing towards maturity amid Westmeath's unploughed meadows, might accomplish. Sadly, he did not live to hear about the two most impressive victories. His fatal heart attack had struck four days before Havago held on doggedly to win the 2-mile Scalp Hurdle at a sticky Leopardstown.

---

* What A Daisy's record as a brood mare was quite outstanding. She produced six winning racehorses in all: Havago, L'Escargot, Red Rossa, What A Buck, The Pilgarlic (another Aintree favourite) and Flitgrove. What A Honey, her daughter with Vulgan, also produced a number of winners, including Wolverhampton, later bought by Bill Davies, Aintree's owner at the time of the 1975 Grand National. What A Daisy died in 1974.

Chapter 3

A peerless judge of horseflesh

The chestnut gelding that had arrived at Gilliamstown in Thomas Matthews's horsebox was moved into the second stable, next door to the yard's latest winner. It was quickly apparent that he had inherited his sire's laid-back temperament. As Jimmy Brogan's daughter, Pamela Morton, recalls: 'If you ever looked over the door, he was always asleep. If not asleep, he was eating.'

Brogan's sudden and untimely death had occurred as the most important part of the jump-racing season was fast approaching. Much as they missed him, his widow Betty and teenage son Barry needed somehow to keep the show on the road. Barry was immediately granted a licence to train, and the mother–son combination kept the operation ticking over, with Barry preparing the horses and choosing the races while Betty took care of the owners. Nine winners were landed in all, while Barry also became – at seventeen – the youngest trainer to saddle a horse in the Grand National.* The relationship between mother and son was somewhat combustible, however. After a few months of working in tandem in this way, Barry left to take up a post with Tom Dreaper, revered trainer of Arkle, Flyingbolt and several other top horses, whose Kilsallaghan base was just a few miles away.

The new chestnut gelding, still unnamed and unbroken, might have dozed his way contentedly through that traumatic year for the yard. On 24 January 1966, though, he appears to have got out of the wrong side of the bed. A handwritten entry in the brisk and business-like farm diary that the Brogans kept reads as follows: 'Escart gld [gelding] had accident on off hind foot'. The entry continues: 'Think he must have galloped into gate. L. Doyle attended, injected anti-bio., anti-tet., dressed foot. £3.3.0.'

Whether that sharp reminder of the propensity of young horses to hurt themselves, even when cosseted, had any bearing on the subsequent decision to sell him that spring is not known. Major Pilkington, the owner who Jimmy Brogan originally thought might have been interested, seems to have been preparing by this time to set up his own small stable in the Cotswolds. With the reputation of Blackrath Stud also rocketing in the wake of the Vulgan gelding Team Spirit's win in the 1964 Grand National, Betty may have reflected, at the

---

* The eleven-year-old Ballygowan had dropped well behind by the time he refused the twentieth fence. The finish was a thrilling duel between the hot favourite Freddie and the Fred Winter-trained Jay Trump, who duly got up to become the first American-bred winner of the great race since Battleship in the year when Jimmy Brogan came third.

end of a harrowing and exhausting twelve months, that the prospect of realising a good price for an unraced younger half-brother to the impressive Havago was simply too good to ignore. Whatever the underlying reasoning, the catalogue for Messrs Goff and Company's annual post-Punchestown sales on 29 April included her three-year-old Escart gelding.

The patch of prime Dublin real estate that the Ballsbridge sales facilities used to occupy encapsulates the way the Irish economy has developed over recent decades. From an adjunct – albeit an exclusive one – of the agricultural sector, the site has gone on to house first a bank headquarters and now the campus of a tech giant. The handsome, octagonal sales building that occupied pride of place there in 1966 could be said to resemble a place of worship to the untutored eye. On that breezy spring day – less than twenty-four hours after another son of a Blackrath stallion, Greek Vulgan, had landed the feature race on the Punchestown card, the Guinness Chase – Mrs Brogan had the satisfaction of seeing her floppy-eared youngster secure the sale's top price. By the time Captain Michael Hall, a vastly experienced auctioneer,* brought down his gavel to signify the end of bidding, the gelding's price tag had risen to 3,000 guineas. It was not a vintage year overall, however. Both the aggregate sum raised and the average price per lot were well below 1965 levels.

The Gilliamstown gelding had been sold to a peerless judge of horseflesh. Tom Cooper was a soft-spoken,

---

* Hall auctioned seven Grand National winners in all: Early Mist (1953), Royal Tan (1954), Mr What (1958), Anglo (1966), Foinavon (1967), Red Alligator (1968) and L'Escargot (1975). According to his son, Robert, he rated L'Escargot the best.

thoughtful and exceptionally intelligent man who had won a scholarship to Trinity College Dublin at the age of fifteen. Among his best friends as he passed through the institution was one Charles Haughey, the future Taoiseach. Having been called to the Irish Bar in November 1949, Cooper served for two years as a barrister on the country's western circuit. His father, a one-time state solicitor of Wexford in Ireland's south-east corner, had trained a few horses though, and bloodstock was the direction in which Tom soon gravitated. By 1966, he was working for BBA (Ireland), the local subsidiary of the British Bloodstock Agency, and had established a formidable reputation, being especially noted for his thorough and indefatigable scrutiny of sales catalogues and the animals to which they related. A profile by journalist Ben Webster in the magazine *Pacemaker Update International* outlines his method and manner. 'The legal training is still evident in Cooper's steady, methodical approach to examining a horse,' Webster writes, 'the unhurried, calm, judicious stare, the logical balancing of the facts of pedigree and conformation.' He goes on: 'Hearing and watching him give his opinion it is easy to imagine him in a court of law... He would have made a generally benevolent judge, but possessing nevertheless a quiet authority and a steely reservoir of severity if the occasion demanded.' The auctioneer Captain Hall's son Robert, the sports broadcaster, remembers that Cooper would only have the horses he was considering buying walked, never trotted. This was because he felt that the animal's walk related closely as a gait to the gallop, and with racehorses it was the gallop that mattered.

As his widow, Valerie Cooper, recalls, he was as soft-spoken in personal as professional life, almost never resorting to bad language, although he could not abide the myna birds that Royal Danieli's jockey Dan Moore used to have flying freely in his family home once he had become one of Ireland's leading trainers. He was also a creature of habit, lunching most days at the Berkeley Court, not far from his office. Unargumentative or not, woe betide any waiter who, unbidden, made so bold as to garnish Cooper's smoked salmon with capers. He was also, as Valerie readily volunteers, a punter. 'I put the form book into his grave because the form book was what he really loved,' she says.

Cooper was not buying Betty Brogan's chestnut gelding for himself. Rather, he was acting for a long-time client, the then US ambassador to Ireland, Raymond Guest.

At this time, the Ballsbridge sales ring was topped by a weather-vane fashioned in honour of a horse called Larkspur. The compact chestnut colt had won the 1962 Epsom Derby in extraordinary circumstances after no fewer than seven runners including favourite Hethersett had crashed out on the famous downhill run to Tattenham Corner. The best part of two years before those sensational events, Cooper had marked Guest's card regarding Larkspur too. His letter to the American, copied out in full in Ben Webster's article, describes the horse as 'about the most flawless individual I have ever seen'. It continues: 'I think he will make on or about 15,000 guineas. At that price he must represent good potential value. As you can see it is a truly Classic pedigree on both sides. I should be very grateful if you would cable me as soon as possible, as if you do not want him we would like to get someone else to buy him to put in training with the O'Briens. I hope it will be you, as I would like to imagine you leading in a Derby winner at Epsom! Yours ever, Tom.' Guest did want him and, after a five-minute bidding duel, he got his way. The price was a lower-than-expected 12,200 guineas – still enough to be reported at the time as the third-highest in Goff's sales history.

Writing after Cooper died following a stroke in 1990, Michael O'Farrell of the *Irish Times* recounted how for years the bloodstock expert had worked with the Ballydoyle syndicate, visiting the main American studs prior to the big summer sales in Saratoga and Keeneland, and reporting his assessments to Vincent O'Brien. 'The success of the great Ballydoyle stables in those halcyon days of the seventies and eighties are in no small measure due to Cooper,' O'Farrell wrote. His successor at BBA (Ireland), Jonathan Irwin, said simply that Cooper had taught him 'absolutely everything about horses and about integrity'. Cooper was, he said, 'the only man I have known within the game who has never had an enemy.'

In February 1970, after the chestnut gelding she sold had become a household name, Betty Brogan received a prestigious Golden Horseshoe Award, presented annually for the horse sold at Goff's deemed to have done most in the previous year for the Irish horse-breeding industry. Pamela Morton still has it, along with a moulded metal snail, retrieved from her mother's Lotus Elan, which was displayed on the bonnet for years as Betty drove around the highways and byways of County Meath.

Chapter 4

Birth of an obsession

Raymond Guest was fifty-eight years old when he bought Betty Brogan's Escart gelding. Tall and silver-haired, he had been acting as US ambassador to Ireland for almost exactly a year. He had been a horseracing enthusiast for much of his life, having acquired his first racehorse in 1931. He also excelled on the polo field, featuring three times in the final of the US Open Polo Championship in the 1930s, in the Templeton team alongside his brother Winston Frederick Churchill Guest, winning twice. Raymond's father, Freddie Guest, a British Cabinet minister and Olympic bronze medallist, and his uncle Ivor, the second Baron Wimborne, played against each other in the annual House of Lords versus Commons polo match at least once.

The family made its fortune from the rocketing demand for iron, and later steel, during the Industrial Revolution. Raymond's great-grandfather, Josiah Guest, turned the Dowlais Ironworks in South Wales into the world's biggest producer of the metal.* Freddie, his father, married one of the

---

* The 'G' of well-known components company GKN stands for Guest.

daughters of Henry Phipps, an American entrepreneur who had been a major shareholder in the Carnegie Steel Company when it was sold in 1901. Raymond was born in New York six years later. After an early childhood spent largely in England, he attended the prestigious Phillips Academy in Massachusetts, where the Presidents George Bush, *père et fils*, were also schooled, as well as St George's School in Rhode Island. He went on to Yale, graduating in 1931, also spending a year at McGill in Montreal.

The Second World War years saw Guest on active service with the US Navy. He worked on minesweepers and was eventually made head of the Navy section of the Office of Strategic Services, the nascent US intelligence agency, in London. The body's European headquarters at the time was at 70 Grosvenor Street, in the middle of what was then the American compound. The Guest family owned a townhouse just off Park Lane, where Raymond would have resided, leaving him with a commute of just a few hundred yards across blacked-out war-time Mayfair. This was a period when the newbie US spies were striving to learn the tricks of the trade at express pace from old hands in Europe. They seem to have succeeded remarkably well. As journalist Malcolm Muggeridge, himself a Second World War intelligence officer, reported: 'They came among us, these aspiring American spy-masters, like innocent girls from a finishing school anxious to learn the seasoned demi-mondaine ways of old practitioners – in this case, the legendary British Secret Service'. Muggeridge went on: 'It turned out that the finishing-school products had learnt all the tricks and devices of the old practitioners in no time at all.'

William Casey, the future US Central Intelligence director, was also based at 70 Grosvenor Street at this time, describing the headquarters as 'bland, grey, non-descript... and heavily-guarded', and London as having the feeling of a city under siege. In his book, *The Secret War Against Hitler*, Casey recalls a 'moment of tension' between himself and lieutenant commander Guest during a meeting in an office where colleagues could occasionally be seen sitting on the floor counting out the contents of bags full of money. Afterwards, Casey was asked to 'try to be nicer to Raymond'. He concludes, 'I must have succeeded because when Raymond Guest went back to Washington in October of 1944, he rented me his family's townhouse on Aldford Street'.

Before he left, chance handed Guest a first opportunity to spend a few days in Ireland. As he later recounted, he had carried the diplomatic pouch to Dublin, staying overnight with Ambassador David Gray at his residence in Phoenix Park. Next morning, Guest transited to Foynes, on the south bank of the Shannon, which had become a major airport during the war, especially for flying boats. 'I found that my seaplane would be delayed for four days,' Guest recalled. 'This was an excellent opportunity for me to visit stud farms and see some horses in County Limerick. I remember going to the Ballykisteen Stud [in County Tipperary] and looking at The Phoenix, sire of so many winners in Ireland.'

Guest entered the family vocation of politics not long after hostilities ended. Running as a Democrat, he won a seat in the Virginia Senate, where he served between 1947 and 1953. A few years later he purchased a stud farm called

Powhatan Plantation in leafy King George County south of a bend in the Potomac river not far from Washington D.C. There, from an attractive, red-brick plantation house overlooking the property, he began to raise horses while poring over the breeding books that held his attention almost as much as they did Tom Cooper's. In 1958 he served as president of the Virginia Thoroughbred Association.

He reconnected with Ireland in 1955, when he sent his horse Virginius to be trained by Vincent O'Brien. The Irishman had just completed a remarkable hat-trick of Grand National wins with three different horses – Early Mist in 1953, Royal Tan in 1954 and Quare Times in 1955. Guest was hoping no doubt that the master of Ballydoyle might be able to coax a similar performance at Aintree from his young gelding.

He had been fascinated by the race, steeplechasing's most arduous test, since his student days. His father, Freddie, had bought a horse called Koko on the eve of the 1928 Grand National. This was one serious racehorse, who had made every yard of running to land the 1926 Cheltenham Gold Cup. Owned by a Belfast linen manufacturer and one-time master of the Westmeath Hounds called Frank Barbour, Koko was also well fancied for the 1926 Grand National but got knocked over at Becher's. According to one account, the horse was jumping 'beautifully' until being 'banged into by Lee Bridge and put on his knees', whereupon he was 'recovering himself quickly' when another horse 'crashed on him and put him out of the race.' Other judges felt that Koko's habit of sometimes skimming low over fences was asking for trouble at Aintree, and in 1927 he sat out both the big English chasing prizes. Still a regular winner, he was back at Prestbury Park the following year, having been moved to a new Barbour stable in Wiltshire, and looked on the point of reclaiming his Gold Cup crown going over the last… only to fade to third on the run-in. The reported explanation was that he had broken a 'small blood vessel'. This did not stop him winning a popular 4-mile chase at Hurst Park, near London, just four days later. It may have been this that convinced Freddie Guest to buy him with the fast-approaching Grand National in mind. The price, paid by Freddie and Alfred Grisar, a Belgian polo player,* was reported to be £4,000 – rather more than Freddie's son paid for the unnamed L'Escargot thirty-eight years later. The canny Barbour also secured a contingency of half the stake in the event of victory in the Aintree marathon. Some weeks earlier, Barbour had sold an even better horse – Easter Hero – under a similarly structured but more expensive deal to another Belgian, the electricity tycoon and financier Alfred Loewenstein.† At the peak of his riches, Loewenstein is thought to have been the world's third-wealthiest individual.

The race, run on 30 March 1928 at a sodden but intermittently sun-streaked Liverpool, was the most melodramatic anyone had seen up to that point in the Grand National's long history. Foinavon-like chaos ensued at the eighth fence, the Canal Turn – in those days an open ditch – when Alfred Loewenstein's recent acquisition, Easter Hero, mistimed his jump, landed on top of the obstacle and slithered slowly back

---

* Grisar is sometimes described as the 'Father of Belgian polo'.
† In 1921, Barbour had sold yet another good chaser, Shaun Spadah, a few days before the Grand National. The horse had gone on to win the race.

into the ditch on the take-off side. Distressed, he ran back and forth across this trench, causing multiple refusals at a barrier that already posed unique questions since runners tackle it while attempting to execute a ninety-degree turn. The wall of horseflesh quickly became impenetrable, and more than a dozen of the forty-two-strong field – a record at the time – were put out of the race. Such was the aftermath that it was decided to do away with the ditch, as it turns out, for good.

This was not, though, where Koko had come unstuck. Widely enough fancied for at least one tipster, the *Northern Whig and Belfast Post*'s 'Goldfinder', to have made him his each-way selection, the new purchase had crashed out once again at Becher's Brook, to the consternation of a small army of punters as well, no doubt, as members of the Guest and Grisar families. Studying footage, it looks like the unfortunate animal, in mid-division, caught the fence and lost all momentum, sending horse and rider plummeting almost straight down over the intimidating drop to a wet, muddy and very heavy landing. So thoroughly stuck did Koko turn out to be that ropes had to be requisitioned hurriedly to winch him to safety.

With so many casualties at the Canal Turn, it was not altogether surprising that, approaching the thirtieth and last fence, only two runners were left standing – Tipperary Tim,[*] an unconsidered outsider whose best days had been thought far behind him, and Billy Barton, an irascible Maryland Hunt Cup winner, trained near Baltimore and carrying, in the

---

[*] The horse was named after Tim Crowe, a talented, early-twentieth-century distance runner from Tipperary.

words of one observer, 'a fortune of dollars', though priced at 33/1. Yet there was still one private calamity to unfold: clearing the last, Billy Barton slipped and unseated, leaving his only rival to plod away to an entirely unexpected victory. The US challenger secured a distant second place after his jockey had the presence of mind to remount, assisted by spectators.

When asked to reminisce about the race in later years, it seemed that the gallant failure of 'our champion jumper', Billy Barton, had ignited the twenty-year-old Raymond Guest's interest at least as much as the misadventures of his father's new horse. Either way, the monstrously dramatic character of those chaotic ten and a half minutes planted the seed of a decades-long obsession.

The question arises, how did the young horse-sport enthusiast – who was studying 3,000 miles away at Yale – actually experience the great race? It is possible, given the family's considerable means, that he joined Freddie and his partner Alfred Grisar at Aintree. The enormous if bedraggled crowd included a two thousand-strong American contingent (as well as King Amanullah of Afghanistan). The atmosphere inside the Adelphi Hotel was such, according to *The New York Times'* man about Liverpool that 'one would think oneself back in America at such a sporting event as the Yale–Harvard football game'. Those who could not be accommodated in the city's full-to-bursting hotels could try their luck on one of three steamships berthed in the docks. (King Amanullah and his wife occupied a suite on the Cunard liner *Scythia*.) In another innovation, the packed racecourse was also served by direct air excursions to and from Croydon, south of London.

A number of twenty-one-seater Armstrong Siddeley biplanes covered the 200 miles in just over two hours. Croydon's new £260,000 aerodrome had opened to business only in January. While Guest would have been quite at home in this throng, I think it is also possible that he remained on the western side of the Atlantic, absorbing the thrills and spills of the great race via another small technological miracle of the jazz era. There were at least nine American-owned runners in the 1928 Grand National. Consequently, US interest in the event was high and an incentive existed to provide the best possible experience for the many US racegoers unable to travel to Liverpool. This 1928 race duly became the first to be broadcast live to a transatlantic radio audience.*

Given the timing, Raymond Guest may well have been among these listeners clustered excitedly around their wireless sets. Freddie Guest only completed the deal to acquire Koko in the very final days leading up to the National. The

---

* The infrastructure involved was of course primitive by today's standards: at the top of Aintree's County Stand an apparatus was rigged up that was capable of transmitting a telephoned commentary, via London and a high-power wireless station at Rugby in the English Midlands, to New York and onwards to the Billy Barton team's home city of Baltimore. A United Press correspondent, C.P. Williamson, travelled to Aintree to provide the commentary. From a perch adjacent to the press box, at the corner of Tattersall's Stand, this would have been a tough task on a day of mist and little sunshine. The very considerable outside noise had to be muffled, a requirement achieved by swaddling Williamson in a blanket. From this vantage point he did his best to follow the intensely dramatic proceedings around the 2-mile circuit with the aid of his field glasses. On arrival in Baltimore, after a fraction of a second's delay, the intrepid correspondent's words were picked up by an announcer and relayed to what the *Irish Times* described as 'thousands of radio listeners throughout the country'.

last two direct sailings scheduled to arrive in Liverpool in time for the off left New York on 17 March; at that time Koko was still Frank Barbour's horse. Of course, young Raymond may have known ahead of time that his father intended to buy a Grand National horse, and planned accordingly, so his presence at Aintree cannot be altogether ruled out.

Regardless, poor Koko was reported to be 'greatly shaken' and 'very stiff' after his ordeal, so much so that he did not run in the Welsh Grand National at Cardiff on 10 April, as originally planned. Nevertheless, both he and Billy Barton were back at Aintree a year later for the equally extraordinary 1929 Grand National. This was the year when a staggering sixty-six horses lined up to start – a record that, thankfully, will not be broken. Freddie Guest expressed an owner's confidence before the race, opining: 'He should win if he stands up.' By this time, however, the eleven-year-old had probably had his fill of racing and was acquiring a reputation as an erratic performer. Sent off at odds of 66/1, he was slowly away and lasted only as far as the first open ditch.

It fell to Virginius to make Raymond Guest's first attempt on a race that still held him in thrall nearly three decades after his father's fruitless efforts to win it with Koko. Like his father, Raymond had chosen chocolate and pale blue, arranged in hoops or horizontal stripes, as his racing colours. This was in large part a tribute to the Churchill family to whom the Guests were related.* The colours of both Sir Winston

---

* Freddie Guest's mother was a daughter of Winston Churchill's grandfather, making Raymond a cousin of the great statesman.

Churchill and his father, Lord Randolph Churchill, were chocolate and pink. As well as polo teammates, Freddie Guest and Winston Churchill were close political allies. In 1921, Freddie succeeded Winston as minister for aviation.

In 1957 Virginius travelled over to nearby Haydock with Royal Tan in good time for the National. To the frustration of connections, he fell at the first fence. 'I thought I would faint,' Guest later recalled. At this point, the Guest family's efforts to land the world's toughest steeplechase could hardly have seemed more futile.

The procurement of Larkspur in 1960 meant that the prime focus of Guest's European racing ambitions switched for a time to that other much-coveted prize, the Epsom Derby. In March 1962, though, following a missed flight and consequent chance visit to the yard run by trainer Dan Moore near Fairyhouse racecourse, Guest decided on a whim to buy a lightly raced six-year-old grey mare under Moore's tutelage called Flying Wild. A striking animal, she would achieve the rare distinction of beating Arkle twice, once in a St Stephen's Day bumper at Leopardstown and once in the Massey Ferguson Gold Cup. Dan Moore's son Arthur, latterly a trainer of distinction in his own right, has described watching that victory at Cheltenham, while a pupil at Downside School, as one of his greatest sporting moments.

Yet, when it came to the Grand National, Flying Wild – like Koko and Virginius – drew a blank. After the 1964 race, Guest might have been forgiven for considering his efforts to win the spring handicap cursed. Sent off at 100/7 joint favourite under future royal jockey David Mould, the mare came down at the first fence, leaving her owner with the unenviable lifetime record of two Grand National runners and zero fences safely negotiated. After proving barren at stud, she did much better in 1966, being pulled up exhausted at the third-last, in going so soft it was described as 'up to your eyebrows' by Tim Norman, the winning jockey. It was just a month later that Guest acquired the three-year-old L'Escargot.

In 1963, Guest's Irish interests became more substantial, with the purchase of Ballygoran Park, near Maynooth in County Kildare, the town where Arkle's owner Anne Duchess of Westminster had her Irish base. The American established a stud on the 335-acre property of unspoilt pastureland and a fine Georgian house with views of the Dublin and Wicklow mountains. Starting from scratch, scores of boxes, a stallion unit and four isolation boxes were built, and fit-for-purpose fencing erected. Tom Cooper had overseen the search for a property, and it was he who managed the stud operation in its early years. Larkspur and later Sir Ivor stood there, with stock from Guest's Virginia farm, such as the stallion Seminole and the mare Pocahontas, taking up residence as the situation demanded.

It was around daffodil season in 1965 when it became known that Guest's profile in Ireland was about to rise considerably higher: he had been nominated as US ambassador in the country. After a Senate Foreign Relations Committee hearing in early March, which dwelt on such weighty matters as Irish sugar exports to the US, Guest was appointed on 11 March and presented his credentials on 28 April. He arrived at Dublin airport with a tightly furled umbrella two days earlier, telling reporters that he thought he had 'landed on my feet' with his first diplomatic posting. There was immediate evidence that the new man was correct in this assessment when Irish President Éamon de Valera brought forward the time of the credential-presentation formalities to facilitate the American's attendance at the Punchestown festival. On a chilly day, sheepskin jackets were out in force and Clusium won the big race, the John Jameson Cup, for the Pilkingtons and Barry Brogan.

Guest's appointment meant that he and his third wife – Caroline Murat, descendant of a king of Naples who had married Napoleon's sister – could take up residence in the stunning eighteenth-century Phoenix Park house, with its big, airy, sun-filled rooms, where he had first stayed some twenty years earlier. A history of art graduate, Guest drew on this expertise to populate the walls with sympathetic artworks, including a portrait of 'an unknown Irishman' by Gilbert Stuart, an artist best known for his paintings of George Washington. At this time, the Phoenix Park racecourse, opened in 1902, was still extremely popular and at one point Guest had three horses in work with Phoenix Park trainer Paddy Kearns.

His stint in his country's diplomatic corps coincided with the calamity of Vietnam. But much of his time was spent on more parochial duties: attending receptions laid on by the likes of the California Raisin Advisory Board one minute, pushing the button to inflate a double-domed nylon pavilion housing the US Atomic Energy Commission's Atoms-in-Action exhibition the next. It being Ireland, and Guest being a traditional all-round sportsman, there was also much to enjoy about the role. What, for example, is not to like about a visit to the Galway oyster festival? Or a trip to a sea-angling event at Killybegs, where he landed an 18lb tope? Or co-hosting a fundraising drive for a new clinic with fellow horseracing enthusiast, the crooner Bing Crosby? Best of all, as his new acquisition L'Escargot was acclimatising to life at Dan Moore's new yard near The Curragh, Guest had the thrill of riding a grey gelding called Shaun to victory at the Dublin Horse Show. 'He was so excited,' Valerie Cooper recalls.

In terms of his horseracing interests, Guest's arrival in Ireland could, it turns out, have been better timed. The very next weekend, his three-year-old, Tom Rolfe, came third under Ron Turcotte* in the Kentucky Derby. Two weeks later, the colt galloped to victory in the Preakness Stakes in Baltimore, second leg of the Triple Crown. It was just two days after the thrill of capturing the Woodlawn Vase, or a silver replica of the famous trophy, that Guest entertained Taoiseach Seán Lemass and other Cabinet ministers at his official welcome reception in the Phoenix Park mansion. If that remained Tom Rolfe's greatest exploit, he had his backers cheering again in June, when he just failed to hang on to his lead in the 1½-mile Belmont Stakes, the Triple Crown finale, which was held in 1965 at Aqueduct. Even at Longchamp in October, where he arrived for the Prix de l'Arc de Triomphe with all his own food, there was a moment coming down the hill when he looked poised to strike. Then, in an instant,

---

* Later known as the great Secretariat's jockey.

the majestic Sea Bird assumed command – 'on the wing,' as Peter O'Sullevan put it.

Yet, being based in Europe did enable Guest to redouble efforts to realise his Grand National ambitions. Flying Wild's return to training meant that for the first time he was double-handed in the 1966 race. A horse called Packed Home joined the grey mare in the ambassador's chocolate-and-pale-blue colours only to come down at Becher's on the first circuit. Packed Home ran again in 1967, Foinavon's year, miraculously emulating the winner in getting through the chaotic twenty-third-fence mêlée at the first time of asking. 'I was more surprised than the horse,' his jockey Tommy Carberry told me, adding: 'It was like the waters of the Red Sea parting.' Unfortunately, approaching the scrum, Packed Home, who had broken a pedal bone, was one of just five runners even further back than Foinavon. While he was among the first to set off in pursuit, the gelding was never going to catch the runaway leader. He hung on courageously to cross the line fifth.* After thirty-nine years, the Guests at last had a Grand National finisher.

---

* Among duties undertaken by Packed Home in his later years was an appearance in a pageant at the Peterborough show.

Chapter 5

Myna birds and sonny boys

The imposing entranceway to Ballysax Manor comes up abruptly beside the road from the M7 motorway in the heart of County Kildare. The walls of the sturdy, two-storey house are not white any more, but the building appears otherwise little changed from the seventeen years or so when it was the base of Dan Moore's training operation. Clipped evergreen hedges and mature trees are still much in evidence behind a beige perimeter wall. St Paul's Church, with its strikingly elongated front door, still stands out on the skyline to the south-east.

Moore moved to the 45-acre property on the edge of The Curragh, about 20 miles south-west of Dublin, in the early 1960s. According to his son Arthur, their original yard just up the road from Fairyhouse racecourse had a 'decent' amount of land attached to it, but this land 'wasn't paying', so they decided to sell up. A clearance auction in May 1964, advertised in the local *Drogheda Independent*, included three Hereford cross cows and an assortment of items – from a Massey Ferguson 65 diesel tractor to a trap harness and a croquet set. Moore sold the property to one of the owners whose horses he was training.

Horses were in Dan Moore's blood. His father, Thomas, was a master of the well-known Ward Union hunt as well as a director of the Hibernian Bank. His mother, Florence or Florrie, was a Smithwick, a family that would go on to dominate US steeplechasing for years in the post-Second World War era through the brothers Paddy* and Mike. The notice of Thomas and Florrie's wedding in June 1906 describes the couple as 'well known in hunting and polo circles', and their wedding gifts included field glasses and three hunting crops.

After education among the Benedictines at Downside School in Somerset, Dan devoted most of his professional life to horseracing, as either jockey or trainer. His exploits in the saddle are perhaps not as well known on the eastern side of the Irish Sea as they might be, since his race-riding career straddled the Second World War. He was good enough, nonetheless, to have been leading National Hunt jockey in Ireland six times. He won all sorts of races. A profile-writer, operating under the pseudonym 'The Toff', recalled how a sequence of wins in so-called 'bumpers' – the 2-mile flat contests that often round out jump-racing cards – once earned him the nickname of 'last race Moore'. Then again, Moore rode the Irish Grand National winner twice in the 1940s, and once – aided by his association with Dorothy Paget, the eccentric

---

* Paddy Smithwick, who died in 1973, was five times US steeplechase jockey champion.

daughter of Lord Queensborough, who owned the great Golden Miller – he landed a four-timer at Cheltenham.*

At Aintree, his agonising near-miss in 1938 remained much the closest he came as a jockey to triumphing in steeplechasing's ultimate test. Royal Danieli failed to complete in two further attempts, while his penultimate effort, riding a horse called Revelry, landed him in the radiology department. His mount became unsighted in the invariably chaotic approach to the first fence and crashed on landing, with another speeding horse then tumbling over him. Moore injured his neck in the fall. Though it was feared he would not be well enough to partner Revelry in the following week's Irish Grand National, in the end he did, winning comfortably. This was also the year when he finished second to Fortina in the Cheltenham Gold Cup aboard Paget's Happy Home.

After the 1947–48 season – having piloted Revelry once again at Aintree, finishing twelfth in the National so nearly won by Jimmy Brogan and First Of The Dandies – he stopped riding and took out a trainer's licence. According to his son, Moore had already to all intents and purposes been training a string of horses for some time, but had not taken out a licence: in those days, race riding and training by the same individual at the same time was not permitted. Moore was able to do this in large part because of what turned into an almost career-long collaboration with a man

---

* This occurred on 22 December 1945, his mounts being Hamlet (3/1), Astrometer (7/4f – and only finisher), Housewarmer (5/6f) and Abbot of Knowle (2/5f).

called Dick O'Connell. O'Connell was a young stable lad in a yard run by Reggie Walker, Royal Danieli's trainer, at the time of their first meeting. In time, he joined Moore at Fairyhouse. The trainer's licence in their yard was in O'Connell's name for part of the 1940s, including 1946 when one of their inmates, Golden View II, won the Irish Grand National and the following year, when Revelry won.* He was still a key member of the Moore team twenty years later when the unbroken L'Escargot arrived at Ballysax. Arthur Moore, who left school and began work in the yard himself after L'Escargot's first season of racing in 1967, remembers O'Connell as a humble man who did not drink or smoke. 'He was part of the furniture,' he says, recalling how he would tell stories about driving Dan's mother into Dublin in a pony and trap. 'She would visit the churches to light candles when my father was riding,' Arthur says.

From that first year in 1949, Dan remained in the upper echelons of Irish-based trainers for three decades. In 1951, the *Irish Times* noted that since he had 'settled down to supervise operations at Old Fairyhouse', everything there had proceeded with 'quiet satisfaction'. There had been no 'spectacular successes', but 'winners have succeeded each other with a pleasant sort of regularity'. Almost inevitably, he acquired something of a reputation as a Fairyhouse

---

* When the *Irish Times* ran a piece in January 1949 introducing Moore as a trainer, it commented: 'He will be helped at Old Fairyhouse by an eminently capable assistant, Dick O'Connell, who knows his business completely.' At this time, there were twenty-five horses in training at the yard, including one rejoicing in the name Sadler's Wells.

specialist, even though he did not officially win an Irish Grand National as a trainer until Tied Cottage triumphed in 1979, at the very end of Moore's career. This is not to suggest that he shied away from new or unusual challenges. In 1954, he became the first Irish trainer to saddle a winner in the USA. This was when three Irish horses were sent to compete in the fifty-seventh International Steeplechase at Belmont Park on a wet day in May on what *The New York Times* described as 'two miles of squishy infield greenery'. Moore's In View could not make the frame in that event, but the horse stayed on in New York and won a $4,000 steeplechase the following week. Moore also had a keen eye for a potential chaser, for example buying the outstanding 1950 Grand National winner Freebooter as a youngster before selling him on to England at a sizeable profit. And he loved Cheltenham, eventually compiling a record of fourteen festival victories, the first of these being Pontage in 1953 in the marathon 4-mile National Hunt Chase.

As of the mid-1960s, however, the Grand National continued to frustrate him. This is best conveyed by the story of Team Spirit, a diminutive son of Vulgan who – rather like Freebooter – Moore had bought as a youngster for 250 guineas. After selling the animal on, he continued to train him, saddling him in three consecutive Grand Nationals between 1960 and 1962, with the best result a ninth-place finish. By this time, the horse was again under new – American – ownership and it was decided to move him to Fulke Walwyn's stable in Lambourn. There, he had two more tilts at Aintree's grand prize, finishing fourth in 1963 and pulling off a heroic and unexpected victory the following year.* The *Irish Times* noted in the wake of the race that it was on Moore's insistence that Team Spirit had been sent to England. The Irish trainer considered that there was 'not a sufficient number of long distance chases for Team Spirit in Ireland,' the newspaper revealed, and 'very sportingly told his patrons that they would get a better return for their outlay by having the little horse permanently based in England'. Be that as it may, Moore would scarcely be human had the result not left him with a twinge of regret and resignation. After all, as *The New York Times* proclaimed, the last US-owned winner of the race had been Battleship, the horse that had literally pipped him at the post twenty-six years earlier. What is more, there had been two other US entries in the 1964 race – and Moore trained both of them. As well as Raymond Guest's Flying Wild, the first-fence casualty, the recently relocated stable sent out the sheepskin-nosebanded Gale Force X – owned by Francis Warrington Gillett, a First World War flying ace – who ran a cracking race before coming down four from home.

In film of Moore in the yard at Ballysax Manor, he has the air of a somewhat dyed-in-the-wool country solicitor, observing proceedings intently in a heavy woollen suit or Burberry-style raincoat and, almost unfailingly, a tie. When he speaks, it is in a slow, considered way, edges rounded by a gentle Irish burr. One imagines a deep, deliberate thinker and

---

* The win provided quick consolation for the defeat of the Walwyn-trained Mill House by Arkle in the 1964 Cheltenham Gold Cup. Mill House's Irish-born jockey, Willie Robinson, rode Team Spirit on all five of his Grand National appearances.

a man little inclined to act on impulse. He inspired loyalty from his staff – whom he referred to indiscriminately as 'sonny boy' – and respect from his peers. Here was a man who, by this point in his life, had acquired the inner strength needed to keep things in perspective, despite the maddening slings and arrows of the racing game.

This steely core beneath the avuncular exterior is not altogether surprising: Moore was a former jump jockey, after all. Not only that, but as a young man he was obliged to spend three years in a brace to rectify a serious back injury. The story goes that the injury was incurred when falling out of a tree as a fourteen-year-old schoolboy but that the problem was not diagnosed for four years. While this did not prevent his subsequent emergence as a race rider, it seems his back continued to trouble him. His son Arthur recalls that he once spent six months at Fairyhouse sleeping on a board, and Dan remembered feeling the vibration from a huge explosion that rocked Dublin in April 1940 while lying there on his back.*

Given the adrenalin buzz that assists jockeys – usually for a finite period – to push thoughts of the dangers inherent in their trade to the back of their minds, it should not come as a shock to learn that there was also an adventurous, even slightly eccentric, side to Moore's character. As well as his free-flying myna birds so disliked by Tom Cooper, one

---

* The *Belfast Telegraph* reported that a 'timed mine' had been exploded at around 5am on 25 April near quarters occupied by Special Branch in Dublin Castle. Many memorial windows in the Chapel Royal were 'blown to pieces and can never be restored'. A member of Special Branch was 'injured by splinters'.

profile-writer noted that Moore was 'haunted' by the number 177. 'Whenever I collect a cloakroom ticket or a racecourse badge, it is sure to be number 177,' he is quoted as saying. 'I am living in hopes that one day I will buy a winning Sweep ticket bearing those magic figures.' He had, moreover, been taught how to fly by Darby Kennedy, an early Aer Lingus pilot,* and, in his later years as a jockey, was known for pitching up at Irish racecourses where he was engaged to ride in a two-seater Miles Messenger aircraft, often accompanied by fellow jockey Martin Molony. He used to navigate with the aid of the roads and railway lines heading towards his destination, and Arthur says jokingly that, if the wind was against Moore on the way to Killarney, the cars on the road he was following would be going faster than he was. This enterprising episode in his career is believed to have ended following a crash landing that damaged the plane.

It was to Moore's new Ballysax fief that Betty Brogan's unbroken chestnut gelding was entrusted after going under the hammer at Ballsbridge. He was to stay for almost a decade.

---

* Kennedy's father bred the undefeated, white-blotched racehorse The Tetrarch.

Chapter 6

A refugee from Sussex

When the three-year-old who was about to become L'Escargot arrived at Ballysax at the start of the England football team's World Cup-winning summer of 1966, a young English amateur jockey called Ben Hanbury was in residence with the Moores. A refugee from Captain Ryan Price's yard in Sussex after the five-times champion trainer temporarily lost his licence,* Hanbury had met Moore in the Irish bar at Cheltenham. Invited to 'come over for a month, sonny boy, and see how you get on,' he ended up staying for three years. He rode a lot of winners and had 'the most wonderful time', criss-crossing the country in his Austin Healey Sprite. Looking back from the vantage point of a successful career as Classic-winning trainer and, more recently, keeper of the impressive equine art collection of the Jockey Club Rooms in Newmarket, Hanbury reflects

---

* Price's four-month ban is examined at length in a *Racing Post* article first published on 8 February 2010: www.racingpost.com/news/controversial-winners-for-ryan-price-came-at-a-heavy-cost/119284.

that 'without the Moores' help and good name, I would not have got where I am today'.

Hanbury remembers breaking the new gelding – the process of getting him used to the tack that would be part and parcel of his racing life, and to the weight of a man on his back – along with Dick O'Connell. 'He was very placid,' he recalls. From beginning to end, this first element of the training regime generally took some three to four weeks of sympathetic and attentive labour, working through a variety of bits, rollers, lunge-ropes and eventually a saddle. The young chestnut's laid-back demeanour was undoubtedly appreciated by his handlers.

The yard routine at this time began around 7am or 7.30am. The standard racehorse diet in those days was oats and bran – even though it has since become widely accepted that, as Arthur Moore puts it, 'it is the wrong race-fuel'. On top of that, twice a week, Moore's horses were given a helping of linseed mash. 'It would bubble up all gluey and gooey,' Arthur remembers. 'Lovely for the horses and their coats.' In time, the future trainer developed his own keen interest in nutrition. 'I started adding soya bean and seaweed meal,' he says.

One of the assets of the Moores' new property was its proximity to The Curragh, an ancient 5,000-acre tract of rough plain and grassland, studded with gorse, exposed to the elements and grazed by thousands of plump Wicklow Cheviot sheep. This was where Dan Moore's strings did the bulk of their exercise, even though it was a bit of a trek to get there. In this way, Ballysax's location meant that the racehorses in his keeping both stayed out much longer than those under the tutelage of many other trainers and got through a good deal of roadwork.

According to Arthur, there were three options as the lines of horses walked out of the front gate in the morning. 'We could go straight on and go for roadwork,' he says. 'Or we could turn left down to an area called the Butts on The Curragh. You had to be a bit careful because the army are based in The Curragh Camp and sometimes they would be shooting there. But there was open land and a good 3- or 4-furlong canter up to the forest. Then you would walk around the back of the forest. There is a lot of rough land you could just do long canters on. Alternatively, if you turned right out of the front gate, it would bring you to the training grounds. You would start off at Maddenstown where there is a gallop... At the top of that gallop you could keep going on and cross the main road and it would bring you across to the schooling ground. We would do that regularly enough – and I would say just to get to the schooling ground was the guts of forty minutes. You would do your work and then hack back again. So it was proper work and [you needed] tough horses to take that.'

The Curragh today is little changed from that period when L'Escargot was being prepared for his racecourse debut. There is more traffic on the roads, no doubt. The sweeping outline of an elegant new grandstand on the eponymous racecourse that is the spiritual home of Irish flat-racing is visible against the skyline as one stands amid the hoof indentations of the training grounds. But those disconcerting military warning signs are as prominent as ever* and the blustery Irish wind whips up just as keenly across the open, uncultivated expanse.

Hanbury retains a vivid memory of one exercise session on The Curragh in particular. It must have been well on into 1966 by this time and, as he tells it, 'I just happened to be put on this horse – L'Escargot. He hadn't really worked before. It was the first time he went to The Curragh… In this gallop – I cannot remember how many horses – he beat them very easily, finished twenty lengths in front.'†

It was unusual for the Englishman to ride the young gelding at exercise. His regular day-to-day rider was Dan's wife Joan, or 'Joanie', an accomplished horsewoman who would often undertake the task wearing one of her collection of brightly coloured silk headscarves. A County Galway native with a piercing gaze that she passed on to her children, it was Joan – along with Mick Ennis, the stable lad who looked after him – who probably established a closer bond with the horse over the years than anyone else. 'He was closest to Joan Moore,' Virginia Guest Valentine, owner Raymond Guest's daughter,

---

* The first permanent military structures on The Curragh were built by British soldiers at the time of the Crimean War in 1855, a year or so after the Charge of the Light Brigade.

† Writer Guy Williams recalls riding along the all-weather track one day beside stable lad Mick Ennis who was aboard L'Escargot. Ennis warned him to drop back when he gave the word that he was about to step up the pace – 'or you'll be off'. As they pulled away from him, Williams noticed that L'Escargot's hind legs had moved out laterally to cover the entire width of the track. 'It was frightening,' he says. 'That was my insight into why the horse was so exceptional.'

concurs. 'He was a funny old boy; I think he preferred women to men,' she says. 'He was sort of a loner.'

Since the horse had attained the age of three without being officially named, it fell to Guest to do the honours. This was a task he took very seriously with the foals produced by his breeding operation in the USA, sometimes drawing on the work of American poet Henry Longfellow. With his new Irish acquisition, he took a different tack. As he explained subsequently, the then US ambassador to Ireland was well aware of the success enjoyed by Havago, his gelding's elder half-brother. 'I wanted to get the name Let's Go,' Guest recounted. Unfortunately, that original choice turned out to be already spoken for. Guest's thoughts turned instead to Escart, the French stallion from which the gelding had been bred. By combining this with part of his original inspiration, he arrived at L'Escargot, French for 'the snail'.

If the chestnut's connections did not already have a pretty shrewd idea of how inadequate, or perhaps ironical, a descriptor of his abilities this would turn out to be, the penny would very soon drop.

Chapter 7

The beating of Garrynagree

By February 1967, L'Escargot had officially turned four and was ready for his racing debut. Proudstown Park, 2 miles outside Navan, not far from the Brogans' Gilliamstown property where he had dozed away his two-year-old days, was the course selected. Navan* was at this time one of the widest tracks in the country, permitting big fields, and twenty-two horses made their way to the start for the final race on that day's card, the Grattan Cup, a 2-mile bumper for runners that had yet to win a race. Neither L'Escargot nor the odds-on favourite Garrynagree – a well-made and speedy individual seen as potentially the next winning-machine to roll off the Dreaper conveyor belt – had competed before, let alone won. With amateur riders called for, Ben Hanbury was wearing Raymond Guest's chocolate-and-pale-blue colours. The race was worth a princely £203.

---

* Navan is where the great Arkle won his first hurdle race, over 3 miles, at a price of 20/1, while paying nearly 50/1 on the Tote. It is also associated with the 1920 Grand National winner Troytown, whose owner was the first chairman of the Navan Racecourse Company.

It was the day after Valentine's Day and this corner of County Meath was cold with a biting wind. The going was soft on a course regarded as a good test of a stayer at the best of times. By 5pm, the scheduled start, it was already too dark to operate the photo-finish equipment.

Well over half a century on, Andrew Kavanagh, Garrynagree's jockey, retains a vivid recollection of the way the contest unfolded. Garrynagree 'went very easily through the race,' he says. 'When I asked him to move up a little bit, he literally took off. You can sit and wait in Navan all day: the last furlong is quite steep. Horses get caught out all the time. I made up too much ground too quickly... I rode a horrific race.'

One suspects Kavanagh might be coming down a touch too hard on himself. The press concentrated on how Garrynagree's conqueror, L'Escargot, had been 'magnificently ridden' by Hanbury. The Dreaper horse 'led in the straight', which stretched over 6 furlongs with a dip in the middle, but – reported the *Irish Field* – 'Mr Hanbury never gave up hope'. Hanbury's abiding memory is expressed in a succinct six words: 'He proceeded to win very easily.' The official winning margin was five lengths.

With L'Escargot priced at a sporting 100/7, this outstanding debut would not have been greeted too warmly by those hardy punters who stuck it out as the evening wind became more bitter and the temperature began to drop. For some, it was merely the final blow on a day to forget, gambling-wise. Not a single clear favourite had delivered that wintry Wednesday, with the shortest-priced winner coming in at 11/4. As Andrew Kavanagh concludes, 'On the day, it was the beating of Garrynagree, not the winning of L'Escargot.' This was by no means the last time that a clear-cut victory by the rangy chestnut with a lick of white on his forehead would be overshadowed as thoughts focused on a beaten opponent.

There was, however, one enthusiastic backer who was pleased as Punch with the Navan upset: Raymond Guest himself. Arthur Moore recalls taking note of the result in a newspaper summary while still a schoolboy in Somerset. 'I didn't probably know the horse's name, but I recognised B. Hanbury,' he remembers. He also recalls that, whether as a result solely of that impressive training-run with Hanbury on The Curragh, or following the accumulation of further evidence of the gelding's potential, connections of the Ballysax yard 'fancied him strongly'. A commission was placed on behalf of Guest with some experienced punters in the north of Ireland, in the hope that this would minimise any cramping of the odds. When L'Escargot cruised home, Moore says that his delighted owner 'wanted to send a car up to collect the money'.

During his long association with horseracing, Guest pulled off some noteworthy betting coups. In Vincent O'Brien's official biography, it is recounted how the American went ahead and backed his 1962 Derby winner Larkspur, in spite of the appearance of a swelling on the colt's near hind leg little more than a week before the race. Even more famously, following his brilliant colt Sir Ivor's first win as a two-year-old, O'Brien describes how Guest 'managed to find William Hill who was on a yacht at Deauville' and place another Derby bet of £500 each way at 100/1 on the horse.*

This second wager was still some months into the future, however, as owner and trainer savoured L'Escargot's bumper success and began to plot the remainder of his 1967 campaign.

The gelding's second outing came five and a half weeks later, the day after Good Friday, just outside the US ambassador's front door in Phoenix Park. As at Navan, there was a chilly wind, which kept the Easter bonnets under wraps. Instead, on the threshold of what was to be labelled the Summer of Love, one fashion-minded reporter noted an abundance of tweed trouser suits in 'swinging colours'. This time, the young horse, again ridden by Ben Hanbury, encountered good going and – in what was described by the *Irish Field* as an 'exciting finish' – lost by a length to an opponent called Irish National, to whom he was conceding 10lb. With the winner beating off a 'renewed challenge' from L'Escargot in the closing stages of the 2-mile trip, Raymond Guest – present in the big crowd along with Tom and Valerie Cooper – would have noted that if his chestnut had lacked a little speed, once again he had not wanted for stamina. The win was one leg of a double for Irish National's trainer Michael Connolly. Back in the field was the Dermot Weld-ridden Ebony King, another four-year-old, who for a time would become a formidable adversary, especially over hurdles. Guest and Dan Moore would not have to wait long for consolation: three days' later their Vulgan's

---

* Claiborne Farm's Bull Hancock bought Sir Ivor on Guest's behalf for $42,000 at the July 1966 yearling sales at Keeneland in Kentucky. He was named after Guest's grandfather.

Prince won a 2-mile chase at Moore's old stomping ground at Fairyhouse. In the last race on that card, Garrynagree won his bumper by a commanding twelve lengths.

A showdown with Tom Dreaper's improving four-year-old took place on the last day of a sunny Punchestown festival just a few miles from L'Escargot's stable on the road to Naas. It was the last week of April, the Kildare gorse blazed a brilliant yellow and the bright spring weather had brought out battalions of large felt hats with floppy brims described by one observer as 'the size of a rhubarb leaf'. The temperature was clement enough for champagne picnics to be consumed Twickenham-style by patrons in the racecourse car park. A persistent breeze and the venue's relatively light, free-draining soil had combined to produce ground that was positively quick.

Dreaper was in fine form, celebrating four winners in all over the three days, the pick of them a chaser called White Abbess, who won the John Jameson Cup under owner Lord Bicester's appreciative gaze. For their second bumper clash, for the Cooltrim Plate, Garrynagree was receiving 5lb from L'Escargot. He duly capitalised to score by three lengths. As winning jockey Val O'Brien recalls: 'I picked it up turning into the straight. L'Escargot came to join on the outside.' Sent off at a price of 8/11, this fourth and final Dreaper festival winner had been widely anticipated.

The Irish Cesarewitch, a 2-mile flat handicap run at The Curragh in October, is a prize that was lifted by several future stars of National Hunt racing in the years following the Second World War. Cottage Rake, Hatton's Grace and Height

O' Fashion all fall into this category. Dan Moore seems to have conceived a notion that L'Escargot might just have the speed and staying power to follow in those illustrious hoof-prints. The stratagem had no real drawbacks: if the feat proved beyond the youngster, he should still improve his stamina and race-craft in making the attempt, and this would stand him in good stead when graduating to hurdles. So it was quickly back into action after his summer break for Ballysax's new protégé. He was dispatched with a small party of stable companions down to County Kerry in the first week of September for the 1mi 5f Carling Black Label Lager Stakes, the feature race on the second day of Tralee's three-day meeting.

Meanwhile, as Raymond Guest continued to fulfil his diplomatic duties, a highlight of his summer had been an increasingly exciting flat-racing season for his horses, crowned by the dramatic improvement being shown by Sir Ivor, the colt he had had bought for him in Kentucky the previous July. In the two-year-old's first race, the 6-furlong Tyros Stakes at The Curragh on Irish Derby day – July 1 – he trailed in a lacklustre sixth, well behind another Guest horse, the Larkspur colt Ballygoran, named after the owner's Irish stud. But less than a month later, on July 29, just after Guest's Arawak had finished third in the Irish Oaks, Sir Ivor forced a narrow victory at the same course in the slightly longer Probationers' Stakes. As the *Irish Times* saw things, the winner 'obviously appreciated the extra furlong'. It was 'only in the last hundred yards that he courageously got to grips with [the leader] Mistigo and stuck his neck out for a narrow victory on the line'. This was the win that triggered that audacious Derby bet – and, as Guest was hoping, it proved a prelude to much more noteworthy victories as the days started to draw in at the approach of autumn.

The Tralee meeting was a jolly affair, coinciding with the Rose of Tralee beauty pageant and held on a course in a former deer park owned by the family of Daniel O'Connell.* But L'Escargot failed to get to grips with a competitive field lured by the valuable sponsored handicap. A five-year-old mare called La Gamberge prevailed, with Dan Moore's representative, a long-odds outsider, in the rear. As after the Eastertide meeting at Phoenix Park, the trainer did not have to nurse his disappointment for long: he saddled the winner in the subsequent 2-mile chase – Neutron II. There was further encouragement for the Moore family on the meeting's final day, when Arthur – back from Downside – rode a horse called King's Sprite to a runner-up spot at a price of 20/1. This was a relationship that was destined to blossom.

It was a week later, again at The Curragh, that Sir Ivor gave the first indication on a racecourse that he could be a Classic contender. On going described as yielding, he won the 7-furlong National Stakes with the greatest of ease. Lester Piggott must have had a good view of this eye-catching performance aboard the horse that finished third. It was, all things considered, a very satisfying September for the US ambassador. The following Saturday, Ballygoran won Leopardstown's Larkspur two-year-old Stakes.

---

* O'Connell was the nineteenth-century political leader of Ireland's Catholics. Joan Moore was a direct descendant of 'The Liberator', as O'Connell was known.

When Sir Ivor next ran in public, it was at swanky Longchamp on the edge of Paris and that man Piggott was on board for the Grand Critérium, France's top race for juveniles. Once again, he won impressively, by a comfortable three lengths. 'Piggott and Sir Ivor rout French,' declared the *Daily Mirror*, making it sound like Agincourt. Piggott described his mount simply as 'one of the best two-year-olds I have ever ridden'.

That was on Sunday 15 October. It was not Guest's sole victory of the weekend. The previous day, another of his horses had carried his colours into the winners' enclosure in the distinctly more homely setting of Naas, just up the road from Ballysax. In the 2mi 1f Rathangan Stakes, featuring seventeen starters – including young Arthur Moore and King's Sprite – L'Escargot hit the front halfway up the straight and held off a late challenge to win by two lengths at 7/2. It was a reassuring return to form and further corroboration of the gelding's deep reserves of stamina. The following week, however, back at The Curragh, he was always well back in the pack in an Irish Cesarewitch run in bright sunshine. The previous day, Ballygoran had beaten only one rival in a seven-runner Dewhurst Stakes at Newmarket. For Guest, it was a salutary reminder of the vagaries of racing.

For Ben Hanbury, who rode L'Escargot to both his victories in that busy first year of learning the rudiments of the game, the success at Naas marked his farewell to the horse and to Ballysax. With Arthur permanently back from Somerset and ready to take on duties at the yard as well as pursuing his own race-riding ambitions, Hanbury returned to England

and set out on a new course as a professional jockey with trainers Roddy Armytage and Ken Cundell. Unfortunately, it was not too long before the capricious gods of racing took a hand. 'I had this terrible fall at Sandown,' he recalls. 'I hit a concrete post and broke my leg very badly. I spent six to nine months either in hospital or a rehabilitation centre in Slough.' On recovery, Hanbury found his way to Newmarket and to top trainer Bernard van Cutsem. As he concludes, 'that was fifty-two years ago and I have never left [the town]'.

As the Englishman took his leave, it was time for L'Escargot to go hurdling and for Arthur to enter what he calls 'the university of life'. First, though, Ballysax Manor – along with the rest of the racing industry in Britain and Ireland – had to face down a new scourge that had materialised just as the 1967 flat-racing season was winding down.

Chapter 8

Champion material

Within days of L'Escargot's moderate Curragh debut, an outbreak of highly infectious foot and mouth disease was diagnosed among pigs on a farm near Oswestry in Shropshire. As the contagion took hold, it forced the mass culling of livestock. And as scientists and officials fought to contain its spread, the epizootic also had a severe impact on horseracing. On 18 November, at the riverside course at Worcester, the first meeting to be lost to the disease was cancelled. By the end of that month, racing in Britain and Ireland had been brought to a complete halt. It did not resume in Ireland until Valentine's Day 1968 when, on a bleak afternoon at Navan, Tom Dreaper returned with a double, and a bright young prospect called French Tan managed to retain his unbeaten record. After such a long break, the size of the fields was described as 'horrifying' by one tipster.

Dan Moore's young star-in-the-making did not make his second-season return for a further two and a half weeks, leaving no margin for error if he was to feature at the Cheltenham festival, towards which all eyes were already turning after that dark, silent winter. The race selected for him was the Osberstown Hurdle, run over 2mi 1f at Naas, the local course where he had already tasted victory the previous autumn. It had been won by some good horses down the years, notably Mill House, Arkle's arch-rival, in 1961.* And on his debut over hurdles, after more than four months unraced, Moore's young apprentice was to produce one of the most eye-catching performances of his career.

There were some tough competitors in the race. These included the hard-galloping Murpep, who had outpaced L'Escargot in finishing runner-up in that pre-hiatus Irish Cesarewitch, Gala Day, described as a 'nice small little chestnut horse' by his jockey Peter McLoughlin, and older campaigners such as Abletai and Razor's Edge. Murpep was very much the punters' choice, but it was Gala Day who led over the first mile in front of an enthusiastic crowd. Murpep then made his move under Stan Murphy, with a horse called Golden Scene, the same age as L'Escargot, making ground from further back. After clearing the penultimate flight, both L'Escargot on the stands side and Golden Scene surged ahead of the favourite. Raymond Guest's horse led over the last, where Golden Scene blundered, leaving the 10/1 shot in the sheepskin noseband to romp home by four lengths. Under the headline 'L'Escargot

---

* A touch ironically, the big horse was ridden that day by Pat Taaffe, Arkle's regular partner. Taaffe left a wonderful account of schooling the young Mill House in his succinct autobiography, *My Life and Arkle's*. 'I hunted him… and he loved every moment of it,' Taaffe wrote. 'Nothing daunted him… And running free across the land, you can believe me he was something to fill the mind of a man.'

Jumps Into Prominence', a photograph in the *Irish Field* shows a rather heavy-looking gelding clearing the last hurdle already well ahead. His overall display was rated 'very polished', while, writing in the *Irish Times*, Michael O'Farrell hazarded the prediction that L'Escargot 'could well make a big name for himself in this game'. The schooling grounds of The Curragh had evidently been put to good use by Moore and his team.

That last-flight photograph also captures L'Escargot's jockey Tommy Carberry, wearing goggles and an expression of sheer determination, in perfect balance as his mount touches down with the race at his mercy. At that very instant, Carberry would have been feeling what one of his main rivals in the weighing room, Terry Biddlecombe, described as the 'positive, heady exhilaration' of knowing you are going to win. This was twenty-six-year-old Carberry's first time up in public on the novice hurdler. No doubt the impressive performance owed much to his aura of calm assurance in the saddle.

Carberry grew up on a farm in Garristown, less than 10 miles from Moore's first training base. The family's roots in the area are exceptionally deep: Tommy's great-grandfather, also called Thomas, is believed to have lived in the same village in the early nineteenth century. Very light as an adolescent, it is thought that Tommy approached Moore in the late 1950s seeking a way into racing. 'Apparently they put him up on a horse and the horse tried to get him off,' says Tommy's son Philip, a Champion Hurdle-winning jockey in his own right. 'But Dad stuck to him very well. They were impressed, but Dad at the time was very light, so Dan sent him to The Curragh to ride on the flat for Jimmy Lenehan.' Progress was so rapid that Carberry was twice champion apprentice, in 1958 and 1959.

The start of his jump-racing career when he was twenty was just as impressive. Riding a horse called Tripacer for Moore in the 1962 Gloucestershire Hurdle at Cheltenham,* Carberry came storming through on the stand rails on the 20/1 shot to beat the favourite by a neck in a photo finish. It was his first win under jumping rules. 'First jump-win and first Cheltenham win both at the same moment,' as Philip economically puts it. He still has an engraved watch given to Tommy by Tripacer's owner, Lady Honor Svejdar, after he won the Galway Hurdle on the horse in the same year.

By the time L'Escargot burst onto the scene, Carberry had added a Massey Ferguson Gold Cup and a Stone's Ginger Wine Chase – both aboard Raymond Guest's mare Flying Wild – to his curriculum vitae, and was well established in the top rank of Irish riders. Like many jockeys of this era, for all his dedication to riding winners, Carberry lived life to the full. His bond with Moore – the source of his big break – was strong and would soon strengthen further: in November 1969, he became engaged to the trainer's daughter Pamela.

It was to the 1968 Gloucestershire Hurdle that L'Escargot was now directed – a logical choice, not least because his half-brother Havago had landed it three years earlier.

While L'Escargot may have jumped into prominence at Naas, other Irish raiders, such as Fort Leney, Herring Gull

---

* Honey End, the Grand National runner-up in Foinavon's year, 1967, was also in the field.

and the still-unbeaten French Tan, were more talked about in the run-up to the festival. This relative obscurity, at least to the English racing fraternity, helped Moore and Carberry to pull off another upset.

Weight of numbers meant that the Gloucestershire Hurdle was split into two separate races, with French Tan included in the first division and L'Escargot the second. Sent on his way with the excited roar that greets the start of the festival curtain-raiser ringing in his ears, French Tan attempted to make all but then ploughed into the penultimate hurdle when coming under pressure. He sustained what was described as a 'super-ficial' cut in the fall. By contrast, Herring Gull won the second race on the card – the Totalisator Champion Novices' Chase – convincingly enough, beating the future Grand National winner Gay Trip, ridden by Biddlecombe, into second place. After one Ballysax horse, Collierstown, with young Arthur Moore riding, had faded to fifth in the 4-mile National Hunt Chase, L'Escargot lined up for the last race of the day.

Biddlecombe was aboard the hot favourite, Pick Me Up, but the pair found themselves caught cold by Carberry's enterprising and supremely confident tactics. As the English jockey subsequently recalled, he thought he would win and 'did not worry unduly when L'Escargot made the running from the start. I had never seen L'Escargot before, nor even heard of him. He was just a horse that had come over from Ireland with very little known about him.' After the Irish 13/2 shot had established a lead of twenty lengths, Biddlecombe took up the chase 'because he showed little sign of coming back to the rest of the field'. But it was already too late. Pick

Me Up closed to within five lengths of the leader on the charge down the Prestbury Park hill, but that was as close as he got. L'Escargot 'set off again up the hill to beat me by six lengths,' Biddlecombe remembered, adding: 'Fred [Rimell, the trainer] was incensed.' It must have been a magnificent moment for the fast-maturing gelding's entourage. If he could perform like that on this most testing of tracks, with its strength-sapping gradients and undulations, what might he not achieve in future? Raymond Guest's daughter Virginia was on hand to lead him in. O'Farrell, the *Irish Times* man, upgraded his prediction, writing: 'There is clearly champion material in this superb horse.' Dan Moore contented himself with informing the world, 'We will keep him hurdling.'

Expectations could scarcely have been higher six weeks later when the chief protagonists of what, despite its delayed start, had turned into a vintage season for novice hurdlers headed for Punchestown. This time they would line up in the same race: the Martin Molony Champion Novice Hurdle. The *Irish Field* labelled it the 'novice hurdling event of the decade'.

There were twelve in the field including Mr Smarty, winner of that 1967 Irish Cesarewitch, and future chasing star Kinloch Brae. But almost all attention was focused on the big three from Cheltenham: L'Escargot, French Tan and French Tan's conqueror, King Cutler. The English-trained horse was based at Denys Smith's yard in Bishop Auckland and would be ridden by Brian Fletcher. This duo had recently won the Grand National with Red Alligator in convincing style. King Cutler was sent off as narrow favourite at 9/4 – ahead of French Tan at 5/2 and L'Escargot 3/1 – even though

L'Escargot's foot-to-the-floor Gloucestershire Hurdle time had been six seconds faster than King Cutler's.

L'Escargot or French Tan – ridden by Cathal Finnegan – would plainly have been capable of setting a fast pace, but neither jockey judged this tactically astute on this occasion. So it was a slow start, with French Tan reluctantly leading Razor's Edge in the early stages. Razor's Edge took over around halfway and then Kinloch Brae took the lead. Approaching the penultimate hurdle, a suitably thrilling finish was in prospect, with five horses – French Tan, Kinloch Brae, the rapidly improving King Cutler, as well as Ebony King and King Candy – in line together. Ebony King touched down first and, with King Cutler making a bad mistake, held his advantage all the way to the line to win by two lengths from King Candy and the big three, with L'Escargot no better than fourth. As at Cheltenham, French Tan returned with a cut, this time above the heel of a hind leg. The first two – priced respectively at 25/1 and 28/1 – were dubbed 'giant-killers', as though they had just claimed a notable victim in the FA Cup. The snail-like start to the race had probably played into their hands. According to Carberry, who had not failed to win on L'Escargot before, 'It was a bad gallop and this spoiled my fellow who met half a dozen hurdles wrong and when they did race he couldn't get going.' But Cheltenham exacts a heavy price, and the fact that all three festival heavyweights had failed to fire suggests this was the real reason for the bookmakers' benefit, even if French Tan had won at Fairyhouse in the interim.

Having said that, Ebony King, who was receiving 10lb or more from each of the favourites, was a fine horse in his own right – and, in Francis Shortt, he had a skilful race-rider on his back. The result also provided a timely fillip for the winner's ailing trainer. As Shortt recalls: 'A fortnight before the race, Paddy Murphy had a heart attack in Mallow races. His wife and myself took over… He won very comfortably. He had everything: stamina, speed, the loveliest jump. He had exactly what you want to win a Champion Hurdle. He was a very good horse. Influenza came at the back end of the year. He caught it and started bursting blood vessels. It spoilt his career. His first race back was at Leopardstown. He wasn't the horse he used to be.'

In the meantime, Raymond Guest's seemingly doomed attempts to win a Grand National had taken a new turn. With no likely candidates sporting his colours as the event loomed in late March, he swooped in to buy the winner of that year's Thyestes Chase, a proving ground for promising staying chasers run in the depths of winter at Gowran Park in County Kilkenny. Great Lark was a nine-year-old mare who up to that point had won six steeplechases. Her chances were talked up in the days before the race. She was said to possess stamina, a good turn of foot, to be 'brave as a lion' and to have only fallen once in covering an aggregate 37 miles in her chasing career. The *Irish Field*, moreover, regarded her as the best-handicapped of the forty-five runners. There was, however, a fatal flaw. This was hinted at by Willie O'Grady, her Thurles-based trainer. Great Lark had 'got the lot', he acknowledged, but 'needs it soft'. In the event, the sun beamed down on Aintree and the going was classified as firm. Great Lark had had her fill by the ninth of thirty daunting obstacles, Valentine's Brook, which she refused when lying towards the rear of the field.* Carberry had seen the writing on the wall almost from the off. 'She fiddled the first and the same thing happened at the second,' he said. '"How far are we going to get?" I thought. She sat on Becher's, slid down and somehow avoided two fallen horses. When she got to Valentine's she just said "No".' One of the stories of the day was the achievement of Guest's fellow Yale alumnus 'Galloping Grandad' Tim Durant in completing the course, aboard Highlandie, at the age of sixty-eight. 'I was an usher at Raymond's wedding,' Durant later recalled. 'And, do you know something, I never had a photograph taken with him in the forty years since – until last Saturday at Aintree.'

L'Escargot's season ended in fresh disappointment at a little after 7pm on 22 May just outside Lisburn to the east of Lough Neagh. In another Carling Black Label-sponsored race, this time a 2-mile novice hurdle at Down Royal, he was sent off as odds-on favourite but went down by a length and a half to the 25/1 shot Isphahan. The handicap provided a good deal of mitigation: Guest's top-weighted gelding was attempting to give no less than 21lb to the winner. Isphahan, who finished strongly up the hill, also had to survive a steward's inquiry.† Tempting as it might be to speculate how many

---

* Her exit from the race, in Guest's chocolate-and-pale-blue colours, can be seen clearly a bit less than three minutes into the excellent British Pathé newsreel of the event, which may be accessed via www.youtube. com/watch?v=CLq9DD-lSto.

† As noted in the *Irish Racing Calendar*, 'The Stewards called for an inquiry into an incident just before the winning post in this race. Having heard evidence from F. Ennis, rider of the winning Isphahan, and T. Carberry, rider of L'Escargot placed second, and Mr T.G. Curtin, trainer of the winner, the stewards decided not to alter the judge's placings.'

punters clocked the fast-finishing outsider and remarked, 'I bet he drinks Carling Black Label', it would be anachronistic: the well-remembered advertising catchphrase did not acquire traction for several more years. What did now seem indisputable was that, after a shortened season in which he had proved his outstanding ability, L'Escargot needed a rest. His owner, for his part, had no shortage of other business on his plate.

Chapter 9

Yellow chrysanthemums and the surgeon's knife

On 29 May 1968, Sir Ivor won the Derby at Epsom with an irresistible finishing burst. Her Majesty Queen Elizabeth II was there. The Duke of Norfolk was there. Raymond Guest's wife Caroline Murat was there, and led the winner in. Raymond Guest, though, was not there. On the afternoon when Lester Piggott – aboard Guest's horse – pulled off what the *Daily Mirror*'s Newsboy described as the 'greatest piece of race riding… ever executed', Guest found himself more than 300 miles away on a tree-covered hillside at Slieve Coillte in County Wexford. He was there for a solemn and moving occasion, one embellished by the verse of Robert Frost and William Butler Yeats, and demanding the presence of Éamon de Valera, Ireland's eighty-five-year-old president, and Jack Lynch, the Taoiseach, as well as the serving US ambassador. It was a ceremony to dedicate a forest and garden-park to the memory of John F. Kennedy, the young US president assassinated nearly five years earlier. The location, near the Kennedy ancestral home, was significant; so was the date on what would have been the slain leader's fifty-first birthday. For all the uniqueness of the event, for all the bred-in-the-bone sense of duty of the ambassador himself, one can well imagine how Guest's heart must have sank when he realised the nature and unavoidability of the calendar clash. Instead of witnessing his colt's heart-stopping final-furlong surge first-hand, caught up amid the colourful throng of Derby day, he was reduced to squinting at a thoughtfully provided television set rigged up with a makeshift cardboard canopy to counter the glare.* Guest made it to London for a champagne party that evening, the night Manchester United won their first European Cup at Wembley. And he was at Epsom for the Oaks on 31 May. But his filly, Stella Negra, finished well down the field in a race won by the French horse La Lagune. It was another reminder that sport writes its own scripts – even when individuals as wealthy and well connected as Guest are doing all they can to influence the storyline.

Guest was very much on the home stretch as ambassador by this point. His resignation – for 'personal reasons' – had been announced on 6 May. He would vacate the Phoenix Park residence by mid-June, following a farewell reception. All too tragically, the Kennedy family would continue to dominate his last few days as a diplomat. On 5 June, John's brother Bobby Kennedy – on the stump for the Democratic Party presidential nomination – was shot. Guest described

---

* Video footage of the occasion may be located at www.aparchive.com.

the assassination as 'just about the worst thing that could have happened to America'.

It was said that Guest was going to return to the US to take an active part in Vice-President Hubert Humphrey's campaign for the nomination and the presidency. But Guest and the Democratic Party had started to drift apart. The rupture came in the wake of the violent scenes that attended the Democratic National Convention in Chicago in August. 'His eyes were full of tear gas,' remembers his daughter, Virginia Guest Valentine. 'When he came home, he said, "This is ridiculous." The next thing I knew he was raising money for Nixon.'

Relinquishment of ambassadorial duties freed Guest up to follow what remained of Sir Ivor's second and final year of racing unencumbered by the demands of international diplomacy.* Surprisingly, the colt proceeded to get beaten at, successively, The Curragh, Sandown and Longchamp, where Vaguely Noble's explosive burst in a Prix de l'Arc de Triomphe attended by Maria Callas, Richard Burton and Elizabeth Taylor left the rest of the field for dead. Sir Ivor did, though, give Guest more cause for celebration before retiring to stud, first in the Champion Stakes at Newmarket then, more remarkably, in the Washington D.C. International, which was run on 11 November – Armistice Day in Europe – at Laurel Park in Maryland. Bursting through to win with a late turn

---

* The ending of Guest's spell as ambassador had another minor consequence for custodians of his Irish horseracing interests: they no longer had to be prepared for him to drop in on them – literally – in his Fairchild Hiller helicopter. This became the property of an entity called Irish Helicopters.

of speed, in spite of the soft ground, he added $100,000 to his career earnings and ensured that he would exit racing with a blanket of laurel leaves and yellow chrysanthemums around his neck. Yet even this moment of triumph had its complications for the horse's delighted owner: *The New York Times* reported that he lost his contact lenses in the excitement following the win and had trouble finding his way to the presentation stand.

While Sir Ivor was making headlines, L'Escargot had been under the surgeon's knife. He underwent a wind operation called a Hobday, introduced to racing by a veterinary surgeon called Jeffrey Brain. 'He would bring them into a field, knock them out and do them in the field,' Arthur Moore recalls. 'You remove the flaps from the larynx to open up the air because the flaps don't open and close, and they are interrupting the intake of air.' As Ben Brain, Jeffrey's son, told me after consulting his father, it was in the early days a labour-intensive if rapid procedure. Patients would be hobbled using leather ropes and manacles attached to the fetlocks. This enabled horses to be dropped on their sides relatively gently onto a bed of straw. To perform the operation, however, the animal would need to be manoeuvred onto its back, requiring further manhandling. In most cases, Ben says, his father could complete the necessary surgery within five minutes. Horses would be sedated, but not fully anaesthetised, using a chemical called chloral hydrate.*

---

* Ben Brain also emphasises that the Hobday procedure is only necessary or beneficial if the horse is suffering from vocal-cord paralysis. He says this condition is rather common.

L'Escargot did not return to the track until late December. Competing for the first time at Leopardstown racecourse in the suburbs of south Dublin, he shouldered top weight in the most valuable race on the post-Christmas card, the Tower Handicap Hurdle over 2mi 3f. It was generally felt that he might need the outing after his seven-month lay-off. And so it proved: prominent early on, the 5/1 shot was hampered and ran out of steam soon after regular jockey Tommy Carberry sought to make a move at the third-last flight. The winner – the favourably handicapped San-Feliu – was receiving 23lb from the Dan Moore-trained gelding. San-Feliu was a decent horse but hardly top class. Earlier in the season, when Moore's horses were showing exceptional form, he had been well beaten at Fairyhouse by another Raymond Guest-owned jumper, Firm Favourite.

Two weeks after his seasonal debut, L'Escargot was better fancied when returning to the same course for the 2-mile Ticknock Handicap Hurdle. In abnormally heavy conditions, the Ballysax resident set a steady pace early on before dropping back into the pack after spreading a plate.* He finished quite strongly, however, staying on well to claim third place just over four lengths behind the winner, French Excuse. All things considered, it was a progressive performance, not least because he was giving the victor 24lb in a mudbath. French Excuse, who was a year older than L'Escargot and had plainly relished the conditions, went on to win the following season's Welsh Grand National for trainer Fred Rimell. It was an

---

* Losing or damaging a shoe.

encouraging afternoon for Moore and Guest: an hour later Firm Favourite beat the up-and-coming Kinloch Brae more than handily in the Dundrum Chase.

It was a disruptive winter weather-wise. On Valentine's Day – a week before L'Escargot's next scheduled outing – Ireland was carpeted with snow. Come the end of the month, someone calculated that Dublin had experienced its second-coldest February since 1947. Frustrated by the frozen ground, the Ballysax operation was obliged to adapt. As Arthur Moore recalls, 'We brought the horses to the beach and stabled them in Baldoyle [a racecourse near the coast north-east of Dublin]. We were able to keep them fit at the beach. We stayed in a bed and breakfast up the road.' One reporter who ventured out to Portmarnock to watch the strings of a number of trainers at work noted that L'Escargot 'did not appreciate the gale blowing in from the sea, and did not fancy standing around just to have his picture taken'. Nevertheless, the burst of seaside training seemed to do the trick – that is, if the outcome of the horse's next race is any guide.

At midday on the eve of the Saturday meeting, there was still snow on the ground in front of the Leopardstown stands. In spite of this, racing was able to proceed as planned, though the ground was described by Michael O'Farrell in the *Irish Times* as 'so appalling… one wonders why racing was held at all'. L'Escargot was entered in the 2-mile Scalp Hurdle, a race that, like the Gloucestershire Hurdle, had been won by his half-brother Havago in 1965. Sharpened by his days on the strand and assisted by more favourable weightings, Guest's fast-maturing gelding simply ran away with it, winning by twelve lengths from the previous year's victor, Muir. A young horse called Leap Frog was among the also-rans in fourth place. It was a seriously impressive performance, even if a photograph of a mud-spattered Carberry clearing the last flight with great care on his sheepskin-nosebanded companion makes it obvious that the conditions were miserable. Half an hour later King's Sprite sprang an upset to beat Garrynagree, Kinloch Brae and French Tan in the Arkle Challenge Cup. Afterwards it was reported that second-placed Kinloch Brae's trainer had been unable to work him on the frost- and snow-bound gallops.

Naturally, the eyes of L'Escargot's trainer Dan Moore and just about everyone else now turned, once again, to Cheltenham. But could his live Champion Hurdle contender realistically challenge the mighty Persian War?

Chapter 10

Losing the Persian War

Arkle's premature retirement in the wake of an injury sustained at Kempton in the last week of 1966 had left jump-racing looking for a new poster boy. One candidate for the role was Persian War, who had stormed to victory in the 1968 Champion Hurdle and would be returning to Cheltenham to defend his crown against L'Escargot and fifteen others. Among the qualities that endeared him to the general public – rather like Freddie, another popular 1960s stalwart – was his fighting spirit. According to journalist and author Robin Oakley, 'If he had been a film star, [Persian War] would have reached the fade-out not with a Martini at his lips and a blonde on his arm but in a blood-stained head bandage.' Here, then, was a veritable Terry Butcher of the equine world, albeit endowed with substantially more pace than the indomitable Ipswich Town and England footballer.

In keeping with character, all had not been going to plan with the Chepstow-trained hurdler's festival preparations. As Oakley recounts, he had fallen and fractured a femur on his seasonal debut, entailing a break from racing of almost three months. Then, a few days after L'Escargot's impressive if mud-spattered Scalp Hurdle win at Leopardstown, Persian War went down to another hugely unexpected defeat, this time at the West Country course of Wincanton. Sent off at odds of 1/4 in the third race of the day, the Kingwell Hurdle, he was beaten by one and a half lengths by a 100/7 shot called Boat Man. What made the upset even more remarkable was that this was Boat Man's second win on consecutive days. Jockey John Buckingham* remembered his surprise on being phoned at six in the morning by Boat Man's trainer and told to drive to Somerset. 'I thought he was mad,' he wrote. 'I didn't fancy my chances against Persian War, but I was upsides him coming to the last and we went away to win the race.' Persian War was not 100 per cent: he had had a temperature on the eve of the meeting, but it had been back to normal on the morning of the race. Trainer Colin Davies later speculated whether an anti-tetanus shot given in response to a cut foot a week or so earlier might have affected the gelding, while his habitual jockey Jimmy Uttley said he had run like a 'dead horse' from halfway. The reverse engendered the odd doubt about the champion's capacity to defend his title twenty days later, with his ante-post price easing from 4/5 to evens. Davies's confidence, however, remained unshaken. 'Don't be misled,' he advised. 'He'll be all right and raring to go.'

After a welcome break in the clouds in early March, atrocious weather set in again as the festival neared. Several

---

* Buckingham was Foinavon's jockey.

meetings were lost owing to waterlogged courses, including two on the Monday of Cheltenham week. Whether or not he was as good as the previous year, Persian War would face conditions contrasting sharply with the firm ground prevailing in 1968. L'Escargot had shown at Leopardstown that he would keep slogging through the deepest mire. As anticipation mounted, the most commonly held view was that, yes, Persian War probably was in good enough shape to win again, but that this could not be guaranteed and, if he wasn't, L'Escargot was the best bet to usurp his throne.

Not surprisingly, Irish tipsters were among the biggest Persian War sceptics. The *Irish Field*'s 'Fleet Street' opined that while the champion would 'beat them all' if he was at his peak, 'the indications that this is not so are too marked to be ignored'. The Wincanton outing, he suggested, 'may well have done him more harm than good'.

Mercifully, the Gloucestershire rain held off sufficiently for the festival to get under way soggily but on schedule. And, at around 4.25pm, those with a stake in a L'Escargot victory were given grounds for real optimism. While, in the words of the *Irish Times*'s Michael O'Farrell, 'eighteen Irish horses wallowed to defeat on desperately heavy going', the lone Irish victor – in the Two-Mile Champion Chase – was none other than the Tom Dreaper-trained Muir, who had finished well behind Ballysax's new star in that sodden Scalp Hurdle the previous month. Among the main graveyards for Irish hopes was the Totalisator Champion Novices' Chase. In a gruelling battle of attrition, both the favourite, the Pat Taaffe-ridden Stonedale, and Raymond Guest's Firm Favourite were pulled up well before the end. The winner was an up-and-coming warrior of National Hunt racing called Spanish Steps. His performance made such an impression on a man called Michael Tanner, watching in a shop window in Putney about 100 miles away, that he went on to pen the horse's biography. The size of the fields once again was exceptional. A Grand National-esque thirty-five runners lined up for the National Hunt Chase. Only four completed the 4-mile course. Last of a score or so of fallers was young Arthur Moore, parting company with a horse called Arctic Ranger.

After a night that had seen a 1,200ft television mast crash to the ground under the weight of ice on a moor in Yorkshire, Persian War and his sixteen rivals lined up for the 2mi 1f slog that would determine the identity of the 1969 champion hurdler. As well as L'Escargot, the previous year's third- and fourth-placed finishers – Black Justice and Sempervivum – were there. So was Ebony King and so were the surprise packages from Wincanton: John Buckingham and Boat Man. Confidence in the champion had not been completely restored, but he remained firm favourite at 6/4. Dan Moore's challenger was seen by the market as the clear alternative pick at 11/2.

It was another Moore – Persian War's stablemate Bobby Moore – who cut out the early pace. A horse called Supermaster briefly took over between the fifth and sixth flights, but the favourite was always prominent with the two main Irish challengers, grinding away on the bottomless ground, handily placed. Much the most significant progress at this stage, however, was being made by the Scottish runner Drumikill. Hitting the front before the seventh jump, Ken Oliver's talented and gritty hurdler was still well clear rounding the turn for home. In the saddle was Barry Brogan, now established as a top British jockey, whose season had included a remarkable five-timer at Wolverhampton four months earlier. Approaching the last, Persian War was finally beginning to erode the deficit, whereupon a mistake by the leader sealed his fate. Were it not for this 'bad blunder', Drumikill's rider later wrote, he was 'certain' his horse would have won. As it was, the defending champion, head down, powered relentlessly up the hill to victory by four lengths and what one newspaper described as an 'Arkle-style reception'. The chestnut gelding who had been dropped off four years earlier at the Brogans' Gilliamstown property could manage no better than sixth.

Uttley maintained he was 'never really worried', while winning owner Henry Alper admitted to taking 'six tranquillisers last night' and trainer Davies discoursed on Persian War's 'gluttonous appetite – he'll eat a mammoth 30lb of oats a day if I let him'. Among L'Escargot's connections, the focus was on their horse's inconsistent hurdling in the strength-sapping conditions. 'He jumped very big and when he didn't he jumped very small,' was the way that Tommy Carberry put it. Looking back, Arthur Moore reflects that L'Escargot 'probably wasn't quite that class'. He goes on: 'He was a chaser. He was always going to be a chaser. He had the stamp of a chaser. It's a different thing a novice hurdle to a champion hurdle.' The acclamation for the first repeat Champion Hurdle winner for a decade and a half had barely died away when Garrynagree, L'Escargot's old bumper rival, tipped up in a new event, the Arkle Challenge Trophy, when he appeared to have the race at his mercy.

L'Escargot was six; the same age as Spanish Steps, Garrynagree and Kinloch Brae, who won the Cathcart Chase with consummate ease on the festival's final day, carrying the yellow and black colours of Anne Duchess of Westminster made famous by Arkle. If the Raymond Guest-owned gelding was to realise his full potential over steeplechase fences, there was no time to lose. And so, less than three weeks after his Champion Hurdle disappointment, L'Escargot was readied for his debut over the larger obstacles. What is more, there would be no learning the ropes on quiet, out-of-the-way courses with few spectators on hand to witness any mishaps. The race chosen by Dan Moore for him to make his bow was the Power Gold Cup, a 2¼-mile chase held directly after the Irish Grand National at Fairyhouse on Easter Monday. This two-day fixture was one of the occasions of the Irish racing year.

Unlike the cavalry charges at Cheltenham, the field would be only eight strong, giving the debutant plenty of room to see and negotiate his fences. The opposition, however, was strong. The very useful Straight Fort represented the Dreaper stable, while King's Sprite and Cnoc Dubh – destined to be purchased by Guest to execute yet another fruitless assault on Aintree – were also present. Most of all, L'Escargot would be up against Kinloch Brae, a wonderfully fluent jumper already viewed as potential Cheltenham Gold Cup-winning material. The Ballysax gelding would be taking them on, moreover, without the benefit of his regular partner in the saddle. Tommy Carberry had not quite recovered from a facial injury sustained when falling from Kilburn at Becher's Brook while well up with the leaders in the Grand National won that year by Highland Wedding. Perennial Irish champion jump jockey Bobby Coonan was, for all that, the best possible stand-in. And he would be in buoyant mood, having just ridden the 10/1 shot Sweet Dreams to Irish Grand National glory. Nor on this occasion would L'Escargot be burdened by the weight of expectation. According to Arthur Moore, the idea was for him to have 'a school around, some experience before going novice chasing'.

Run on fast ground that could hardly have been more different from that encountered earlier in the season, the race was just about perfect from an educational perspective: it turned quickly into a procession, with Raymond Guest's horse, untroubled by bumping and barging, able to go along at his own pace with all the time and space he needed to size up the unfamiliar obstacles. But it also underlined how much progress he would need to make to be competitive against the best chasers around. Kinloch Brae's jockey Timmy Hyde remembers that he won the race 'very easily', a succinct and accurate assessment. The 6/4 favourite took an immediate lead, as L'Escargot bided his time in fifth place. Dan Moore's charge had cruised up to third by halfway, at which point Hyde opened the throttle just a touch, quickly establishing a fifteen- to twenty-length advantage. Having kept company with Straight Fort for a while, L'Escargot pulled clear into a comfortable second place at the fourth fence from home. He passed the winning-post even further ahead of Straight Fort than Hyde and Kinloch Brae were ahead of him. Though it was not a contest to set pulses racing, the winner, who was giving L'Escargot 12lb, was said to have got 'the biggest reception of the day'. This may in part have reflected his status as the only winning favourite on the card. But this was a public who knew quality when they saw it. Writing in the *Irish Field*, Dave Baker paid Kinloch Brae the ultimate accolade, describing the way the horse decked in yellow and black treated his rivals as 'reminiscent of Arkle at his zenith'. As for L'Escargot, well, it added up to a perfectly adequate debut in the new format.

The gelding's education continued with two more relatively gentle springtime tests, both of which he passed with flying colours, before his principals dispatched him on an altogether more demanding, and highly unusual, summer adventure.

May Day saw him back at Punchestown, a course on which he had so far delivered only disappointment for his handlers. This time, though, the auguries were good. The Moores had already tasted success at the three-day meeting, which had got under way on 29 April. Dan had saddled two winners, including the classy Veuve, who had won the Martin Molony Champion Novice Hurdle where L'Escargot had flopped the year before. Arthur for his part had ridden King's Sprite to victory in the John Jameson Cup – a contest in which L'Escargot would have stood every chance, as the *Irish Field* remarked, had his trainer opted to expose him to a sterner examination. Instead, the apprentice lined up with just four other runners for the 2-mile Colliers Chase. Here his main rival would be Twigairy, another Anne Duchess of Westminster-owned horse. Reunited with Carberry and in receipt of 5lb from his Tom Dreaper-trained adversary, L'Escargot was sent off as odds-on favourite. He duly delivered with what one newspaper described as 'the minimum of fuss', taking the verdict by six lengths. Carberry played a waiting game, hitting the front only at the third-last and sailing decisively away after Twigairy had fought back to join him at the next obstacle.

Eleven days later, this time at Leopardstown* and in a marginally longer contest, the Woodbine Chase, on softer ground, history broadly repeated itself. In another five-horse race, once again featuring Twigairy and again at odds-on, even though he would this time be giving his chief rival 3lb, L'Escargot won even more easily. Pundits attending the evening meeting were seriously impressed. 'He jumped with precision throughout and quickened whenever asked, the prerequisites of a good chaser,' purred the *Irish Field*. On this occasion, L'Escargot's superior jumping had put him in control of proceedings by halfway. Twigairy then got within a length of the long-time leader a couple of fences from home. But rider Pat Taaffe's efforts, as he must always have suspected, were in vain. Sensing the looming presence, Carberry simply let out his reins and allowed his mount to coast away, opening up an eight-length margin.

It was the nearest thing the sport of steeplechasing offers to a formality. But for horse and rider there would soon be stiffer and more exotic challenges.

---

* The highly competitive handicap hurdle that followed L'Escargot's race was won in fine style by a young Glencaraig Lady.

Chapter 11

A whiff of Gatsby

Belmont Park is a colossus of a horseracing venue about 15 miles east of Lower Manhattan at the western end of Long Island. It opened in 1905 and is famous for its sweeping, 1½-mile dirt track that hosts the Belmont Stakes, third and last leg of the Triple Crown.* In 1969, it was also still staging steeplechase races. This was where L'Escargot was to have his next outing.

Air transport had come on leaps and bounds since Dan Moore took In View to Belmont in 1954. And with his flat-racing interests in Ireland and Virginia, Raymond Guest was growing accustomed to the rigours and rituals of transatlantic travel for man and beast. Nevertheless, this was a highly unusual raid for a jump racer, even if the concept of internationalisation was starting to gain traction. Guest had been elected president of the United Hunts Racing Association as early as 1936. He would soon embark on an eight-year stint

---

*   Most notably, this is where Secretariat streaked to his crushing thirty-one-length victory in the 1973 Belmont Stakes.

as chairman of the USA-based National Steeplechase and Hunt Association. It seems natural to think that much of the impetus for this trek to the New York suburbs by his rising star came from him. Moore had his own family connections and past experience at the track to draw on. Moreover, if the gelding proved up to the novel test, it would speed his development as a chaser and help him raise his game to the level of Kinloch Brae and one or two others. Plus, of course, American prize money was generous by British and Irish standards.

The venue was much changed from the 1950s, even if a whiff of Gatsby still hung about the place. For much of the 1960s, it had been closed while the old grandstand was replaced. But in May 1968 a towering new $30million structure was opened, with the snip of a green and white ribbon by a pair of gold scissors, while L'Escargot was still novice hurdling. Just over a year later, and a mere three weeks after outclassing Twigairy at Leopardstown, Guest's horse lined up with eleven other starters for the fifty-third running of the Meadow Brook Steeplechase Handicap. Fifteen years earlier a near-namesake, Escargot, had run up a streak of seven straight victories on tracks in the eastern USA. Were any of the 22,000 spectators at Belmont that day reminded of this as they studied their racecards or queued for clam chowder? It would be nice to think so.

According to an account of the race in the 1969 edition of John E. Cooper's *Steeplechasing in America*, L'Escargot had arrived in the USA only a few days earlier. What is more, he was 'supposed to jump too big and too slowly to successfully compete with American brush horses'. Cooper goes on: 'He did just that for a fence or two and then settled down to the serious business of flying the brush.' On turf classified as soft in spite of the sunshine bathing proceedings, the Irish challenger was well placed throughout, looming up behind the tiring leader, a mare called Free Romance, as the final stages of the 2½-mile trip approached. If Tommy Carberry thought for a second that the race was his for the taking there and then, he was swiftly disabused of the notion when an eight-year-old called Wanderlure came powering through on the outside to lead going over the last fence. In a frantic finish, the dogged L'Escargot, carrying 10st 8lb, was handed his chance when Wanderlure started to hang. Even then it was not over: an outsider called Rural Riot stormed up on L'Escargot's inside. It took 'strong handling' by Carberry, operating like other riders with his mount's number displayed on an armband as well as the saddle-cloth, to hold off the final challenge and win by a head. The Guests were on hand to receive the trophy, along with a satisfied Dan Moore. A photograph from the winners' circle shows Carberry beaming, L'Escargot with ears pricked and Joan Moore in sunglasses keeping a close eye on proceedings. This battling win 3,000 miles from home completed what turned out to be the only hat-trick of L'Escargot's career. It was worth $15,405 – much the largest purse he had yet earned.

The original intention was for this to have been the first of a two-pronged summer assault on some of US steeplechasing's richest prizes by this increasingly impressive performer. The second target was the $35,000 American Grand National, run over 3 miles, again at Belmont, just nine days later. This plan was scuppered when L'Escargot was found to be lame just before the race. A *New York Times* report notes simply that L'Escargot, the 'program favorite, was a late scratch'. In his absence, the race was won by a five-year-old called High Patches. Curator and Free Romance – placed fourth and fifth respectively in that recent Meadow Brook Chase – finished third and fourth.

The Irish horse and his connections were down but not out. Four months later, they returned to the Big Apple – and this time their eyes were on an even bigger prize.

The Temple Gwathmey Steeplechase Handicap* does not trace its origins to either a religious sect or a masonic lodge. Its arresting name is a tribute to one James Temple Gwathmey, an amateur jockey with business interests in the cotton industry, who used to race horses in a partnership called Mr Cotton. In 1969, it was the richest jump race in the USA. The prize of just over $38,000 that it was worth to that year's winner was comparable to the sum Gay Trip would earn by winning the 1970 Grand National at Aintree.

On 17 October – a day when, on the other side of the Atlantic at Kempton Park, only two horses went to post for a race called the Koko Handicap Chase – L'Escargot was once again in a field of twelve beneath that towering Belmont grandstand. This time he was a known quantity and was sent off as favourite, in spite of giving 20lb to the race's light-weight, Somaten, a six-year-old gelding from Uruguay owned by a Long Island attorney. The ground was firm and the trip 3 miles – the first time the Irish raider had raced over this

---

* Unlike the Meadow Brook, the Temple Gwathmey is still run, at Middleburg in Virginia.

distance. For much of the duration, Carberry tracked the pacemaker and top weight, Jacko, until the leader cracked on the approach to the last fence. At this point, the race flared into life, with L'Escargot and the fast-improving Somaten bursting through to take the obstacle almost together. According to John E. Cooper's report, the pair 'brushed' on landing, with L'Escargot 'seeming to come off second best'. Somaten was away and ran on to win by three lengths, while another fast finisher, Lake Delaware, surged into the picture on the extreme outside. In the dash for the line, the American horse won the verdict by a nose. Reported Cooper, 'it took the placing judges some minutes to decide the finish'.

Whether or not this gave Dan Moore flashbacks to the 1938 Grand National, it was not the result he and Guest had been hoping for. L'Escargot's owner nonetheless picked up $6,000 for the horse's third-place finish, and there would be further recognition of their imagination and efforts when L'Escargot was voted the 1969 US Steeplechase Horse of the Year, largely on the strength of his Meadow Brook victory. Both Moore and Guest had the satisfaction of knowing, moreover, that the gelding would be returning to a busy winter in Britain and Ireland far more race-hardened than before his first transatlantic jaunt in June.

The Irish horse and his connections would be back in America the following year, lured by an even bigger purse. Now, though, it was time to refocus attention on contests closer to home – in particular a bold new experiment that was being brought to fruition with the help of one of the racing industry's cigarette sponsors.

Chapter 12

It's a knock-out

Many sports have sought to draw lessons from association football's unique global success story. Horseracing provides an early example. With sponsorship money pouring into the sport – mainly from the drinks and tobacco industries – as the prosperous and socially transformative decade of the 1960s neared its end, innovation was in the air. Nowhere was this more apparent than at the Lancashire racecourse of Haydock Park, between Liverpool and Manchester, just a few hundred yards off the new M6 motorway.

The clerk of the course at this time was a man called John Hughes. He was credited with a new plan to combine the thrills and spills of novice chasing with elements of the exciting knock-out cup format familiar to fans of football and other team sports. The desired result was to get turnstiles clicking both at his racecourse and others across the country from Taunton to Ayr. A number of regional qualifying races, or heats, would be staged around Britain and Ireland from each of which the first four past the winning-post would qualify for a grand final to be run at Haydock. The tobacco company W.D. & H.O. Wills was persuaded to stump up £13,000 in backing, and the stage was set for the most valuable day's racing in the history of the seventy-year-old venue. As Hughes explained to the *Coventry Evening Telegraph* journalist Reg Mackinnon, 'One of the ideas behind this series of races is that people will become partisan to their own home horse, as they are to their local football team, and that they will make up parties to come and see the final.' Conveniently for Haydock, the racecourse was nestled in a football enclave, with four of the country's biggest clubs within 25 miles of its stiff steeplechase fences.

The Irish qualifier was set to take place at Punchestown less than a month after the Temple Gwathmey on 15 November. Two trainers – Tom Dreaper and Dan Moore – accounted for more than half of the eleven-strong field that came under starter's orders for the 2½-mile Sandymount Chase. Moore's representatives were L'Escargot, the top weight and odds-on favourite, ridden as usual by Tommy Carberry, whose engagement to the trainer's daughter Pamela had been announced that week in the *Irish Times*, and Trentina, another Raymond Guest-owned chaser, who would have Moore's son – Carberry's future brother-in-law – Arthur in the saddle. It turned out to be an eventful race from early on. After just three fences, Dreaper's representation had been reduced by 50 per cent, Fortina's Dream falling and bringing down Twigairy. The other two Dreaper horses were already leading the way, with Moore's duo on their heels. This was the situation until halfway, when the mare Trentina crashed out, leaving East Bound, Proud Tarquin and L'Escargot well clear. L'Escargot looked to have plenty in reserve before making errors at both the fourth-last and the third-last fences and dropping back. The surviving Dreaper duo now had the race between them, but at the penultimate obstacle Proud Tarquin – a half-brother of the 1968 Cheltenham Gold Cup winner Fort Leney – took a tumble. The race was consequently East Bound's – if he jumped the last. This was no mere formality since, as Proud Tarquin's jockey Peter McLoughlin told me, his riderless horse nearly took his stablemate out. That really would have been a disaster for the Kilsallaghan operation. Happily, the leader's jockey, Sean Barker, dealt with the situation and cruised over the line, with L'Escargot still ten lengths back in second place. This was not, all things considered, the worst result for the Ballysax team: as a heat winner, East Bound would carry 5lb more than L'Escargot in the Haydock showdown; here, by contrast, Guest's gelding had been giving his rival no less than 21lb. You could view it as a design flaw of the new series.

L'Escargot's name was at this stage still associated with another valuable new addition to the winter racing scene, the Irish Sweeps Hurdle. At the first acceptance stage in early December, he was one of thirty potential runners declared. These included Persian War and other big guns of British hurdling. It was at this point, however, that Moore's plans for his hottest property threatened to unravel.

Outbreaks of equine coughing had been troubling racing for months, and as the industry began to focus on the big yuletide meetings, the malady penetrated Ballysax. For a short time, the situation appeared bleak; L'Escargot was with-drawn from the Sweeps Hurdle and on 13 December it was reported that one leading bookmaker had taken him out of the betting for the big Haydock finale for which he had qual-ified at Punchestown, the Wills Premier Novices Chase. In L'Escargot's case, thankfully, the alarm proved short-lived. His preparations were soon back on track, with a return to action planned for the day before the star-studded hurdle at Fairyhouse in the comparatively low-profile Paddock Handicap Chase. The St Stephen's Day race would bring him back into opposition with his old bumper rival Garrynagree. Perhaps owing to the weights, which required Moore's soon-to-be seven-year-old to concede 9lb to a very good horse, or perhaps owing to lingering doubts about his full fitness, L'Escargot was sent off very much second-favourite at 11/4, against Garrynagree's 11/10.

There was a good omen earlier in the afternoon when Moore and Guest's Trentina beat the odds-on Proud Tarquin in the Irish Independent Cup. This turned out to be a relia-ble augury. The *Irish Field* reported that Trentina's stablemate 'showed all his old verve' in pulling off a comfortable victory. Perhaps unsure himself of his mount's stamina, Carberry played a waiting game, permitting Garrynagree to move several lengths clear just after halfway in the 2¼-mile contest, before reeling him in with four fences to go. As he grew older and more experienced, L'Escargot was also observed to be developing the habit of lifting his head up when hitting the front, making the run-in more arduous than it needed to be and potentially letting victories slip. This might explain why the tactically astute Carberry was content to track his main rival prior to outjumping him at the last, with the winter sun flashing off his mount's chestnut flanks. The margin at the finishing-post was three lengths. All doubts regarding his capacity to scoop the big prize in Lancashire on 17 January had seemingly been banished.

The following day, Terry Biddlecombe, hugging a tight inside line, in spite of the 'huge hurdles which to me resembled gates', swooped to land the £10,000 Irish Sweeps Hurdle on the 1969 Cheltenham festival winner Normandy. Persian War, accidentally caught by Biddlecombe's whip in the frantic closing stages, could manage only third. As a four-year-old, Normandy was receiving weight from most of the fourteen other runners, who included French Tan and Leap Frog. Carberry trailed in down the field riding Boat Man, the horse that had shocked Persian War at Wincanton earlier in the year. Half an hour later, Kinloch Brae eased to another hugely impressive victory in the Christmas Chase.

If Moore was now hoping for a trouble-free countdown to the big day at Haydock, he was destined to be disappointed. A mere forty-eight hours into the new decade, temperatures plunged. Among a string of abandoned fixtures was the meeting at Naas at which L'Escargot was to have had his final run-out, in the Boyne Handicap Chase. His trainer, though, appeared unperturbed, remarking on what an easy horse he was to get ready and how he could 'keep him on the move'. If need be, the yard could always relocate once again to Baldoyle and the wintry Irish coast. But, Moore emphasised, he would only think of returning him to Portmarnock 'if the weather conditions worsen'. There was also the risk that Haydock itself might have to be abandoned; less than a week before L'Escargot was due to fly to Manchester, the course was still covered in snow. Fortunately, in the nick of time, the frosts relented. Following an impressive pre-departure schooling session at Punchestown, Moore was brimming with confidence. 'It would take something sensational for my fellow to be beaten at Haydock,' he maintained. 'I am sure that bar an accident he will win.'

Other than East Bound, whom he would be meeting on dramatically better terms than at Punchestown, the main danger to L'Escargot in the seventeen-strong field that assembled at Haydock was thought to be Royal Relief, a talented stablemate of Spanish Steps from Edward Courage's yard near Banbury. Royal Relief had won the Warwick qualifier with ease. He would be ridden at Haydock by Josh Gifford, the four-time champion jockey who was a particularly good judge of pace. Then again, as the *Irish Field* commented, every single runner had winning form that season. In such a crowded and classy field, the Irish horse's starting price of 9/4 appeared none too generous.

Stan Murphy set the pace on a comparative veteran called Final Move who had won five early-season races in a row. Sean Barker on East Bound and Young Ash Leaf, the main Scottish challenger carrying Peter Ennis, were careful not to let the outsider get away, however, while Carberry and Gifford bided their time. Young Ash Leaf hit the front after the seventh fence, by which time the contest was already over for three of the field, including the well-fancied Bay Tarquin.

There was further drama at the eighth, where Great Noise went down, badly hampering the 9/1 shot Roman Holiday, an outstandingly fluent jumper, and the outsider Saccone. Going down the back straight, Carberry had manoeuvred L'Escargot up into third place, but Royal Relief had lengthened his stride and was coming dangerously into the picture. With East Bound leading over the penultimate fence, an exciting finish appeared to be in prospect. The going was soft, though, after absorbing so much recent moisture, and the Courage horse had the misfortune to slip on landing. While Gifford clung on, his momentum was lost. Although Young Ash Leaf was keeping going, the contest now looked to be between the two Irish challengers. Well aware of his weight advantage, Carberry held his mount in check until the last fence where, for the first time, he took the lead. Barker drove on strongly but could get no closer than two lengths, holding off Young Ash Leaf by only a neck.

Moore and Guest were left to celebrate another big prize of just under £4,500. In an absorbing day's racing, Persian War suffered another setback, swallowing his tongue during a highly competitive handicap hurdle and finishing down the field. With his star chaser having justified his confidence in such impressive style, it was not long before Dan Moore confirmed that his next major target would be the most ambitious yet. L'Escargot's next visit to Cheltenham in March would see him take a tilt at the festival's most coveted prize, the Gold Cup. There seemed little doubt that this would stretch the gelding to his utmost: quite apart from the calibre of the opposition, he would once again be required to race over a longer distance – 3¼ miles – than he had encountered before. What is more, unlike Haydock, the Gold Cup was run at level weights. Yet Moore insisted that he had 'had the Gold Cup in mind for L'Escargot since he began chasing last year'. To which a valid response might have been: 'Yes, but did you have in mind the *1970* Gold Cup?'

The wisdom – or otherwise – of the decision would become clear soon enough. First, there was the rest of a muddy winter to slog through.

Chapter 13

A changing of the guard

The frost and snow that had disrupted January's fixtures was not finished with racing yet. In mid-February, another cold snap descended. Among the victims was the Fairyhouse meeting at which Kinloch Brae – widely seen as Ireland's leading hope for Cheltenham Gold Cup glory – was to have run in the Scalp Hurdle, won by L'Escargot at Leopardstown in atrocious conditions the previous year. Kinloch Brae's trainer, Willie O'Grady, reported ground so hard in County Tipperary that 'we could not even bring Kinloch Brae out for a trot'. The Anne Duchess of Westminster-owned horse would eventually have his final preparation for Cheltenham at his local course, Thurles, in early March. He duly cruised to victory in the 2½-mile PZ Mower Power Chase at odds of 1/3. His performance was described inevitably as 'worthy of the great Arkle'.

L'Escargot's big-race build-up was both less disrupted and, most would have argued, decidedly less impressive. His only outing before returning to Cheltenham, in the 3-mile

Leopardstown Chase, survived the renewed freeze – just – but he was soundly beaten. The race was staged at Navan while its eponymous home underwent an extensive million-pound facelift. Conditions were comparable to that dreadful afternoon at Leopardstown almost exactly a year earlier, when Raymond Guest's chestnut gelding ran away with the Scalp Hurdle. The ground at Navan was so deep as to render the 11st 13lb that he would be carrying a particularly severe imposition. Even so, in light of his Haydock heroics, he was sent off as a warm, if not red-hot, 6/4 favourite. Setting off in heavy rain and buffeted by a strong wind, it did not take long for a horse called Enda's Choice – ridden by the popular Francis Shortt and carrying an almighty 34lb less than L'Escargot – to build up a big lead. This partnership was still going strong the first time they galloped past the stands, raising a good-natured cheer, and indeed 2 miles had been covered, with Tommy Carberry nursing L'Escargot towards the back of the field, before the gap began inexorably to shrink. By this point, the nine-year-old King Vulgan, who had never won a steeplechase in his life, was improving rapidly, with Carberry attempting to push his mount along in his wake. Four fences from home, King Vulgan took over at the head of proceedings and, with his 22lb weight advantage over the favourite, quite simply never looked like being reeled in. In the words of the *Irish Field*'s man on the spot, the leader 'turned the race into a procession', with L'Escargot struggling successfully to cling on to second spot fifteen lengths behind.

It was hardly surprising after these two performances that Irish talk around the Gold Cup tended to concentrate even more heavily on Kinloch Brae. But there was a direct point of comparison in the shape of Herring Gull, a more than useful chaser who was another likely Cheltenham Gold Cup starter. He had run against L'Escargot at Navan and against Kinloch Brae at Thurles. In that storm-tossed Leopardstown Chase he had had to hump around 1lb more even than Ballysax's star turn but had performed significantly worse. Against Kinloch Brae on better ground in a shorter contest, he had gone in at level weights and been beaten by ten lengths. This could be interpreted as offering hope that L'Escargot had at least improved relative to his O'Grady-trained rival since the chestnut's first outing over fences, when they had last crossed swords. His Navan showing had also rubbed out the question-mark over his capacity to stay over 3¼ miles in the Cotswolds. This was a point underlined a few days later by Joan Moore. 'L'Escargot will be sent to Cheltenham and he must have a very good chance of finishing in the first three,' she said, adding: 'He is fit and well after his run in the Leopardstown Chase where he proved he can stay 3 miles.'

L'Escargot had also had something of a symbolic victory over Kinloch Brae by scooping another award linked to his exploits in 1969. The Irish Racing Writers voted him the horse that, having been sold at Goff's, did most in the course of the year to advertise Irish breeding. Second was the dual 2,000 Guineas winner at both Newmarket and The Curragh, Right Tack, and third was Kinloch Brae. As L'Escargot's vendor, this entitled Betty Brogan to be presented with the 'Goff's Golden Horseshoe Award' at an early-March reception in Dublin. It remains in the possession of the family.

The 1969–70 season might have been dreary and more than a little challenging weather-wise, but it had produced some exhilarating racing. As another Cheltenham festival drew near, while Persian War seemed well set to retain his hurdles crown in spite of some high-profile defeats, the main steeplechasing events looked wide open. A changing of the guard was taking place. This had been on the cards: the winners of both the previous season's Cheltenham Gold Cup and Grand National had been twelve-year-olds.* Moreover, Fort Leney, the 1968 Gold Cup winner, had been retired. What was both less foreseeable and extremely exciting for racegoers was the sheer number of young pretenders to have emerged. In England, Spanish Steps had followed up his 1969 Cheltenham festival victory by winning the Hennessy Cognac Gold Cup at Newbury. The powerfully built Courage chaser was one of three Gold Cup starters trying to extend runs of three wins on the spin. Titus Oates, trained by the prolific ex-jockey Gordon Richards, who had taken both the Massey Ferguson Gold Cup, staged at Cheltenham, and Kempton's King George VI Chase, was another. The third was Irish-based French Tan, who most recently had travelled to Ascot for a valuable handicap and waltzed away with the race by ten lengths. One horse – Kinloch Brae – would be trying to extend a run of four wins on the spin. This quartet alone would have provided the wherewithal for quite some championship. Add to that two chalk-and-cheese Vulgan offspring – the tiny Gay Trip and the up-and-coming giant The Dikler – plus the

---

* What A Myth and Highland Wedding respectively.

ever-classy The Laird, the dual Whitbread Gold Cup-winning veteran Larbawn, and a 33/1 shot called L'Escargot and you had the ingredients for a stone-cold classic.

The festival's first day fell on 17 March – St Patrick's Day – and what a day it was for the Irish. On this occasion, the first race was the Two-Mile Champion Chase and, in a terrific contest run on good ground, the Tom Dreaper-trained Straight Fort ridden by Pat Taaffe just held off L'Escargot's rival from Haydock, Royal Relief. The winner was greeted not only by seemingly half the population of Ireland, but also by an Aer Lingus cabin attendant carrying a basket of shamrock, to which Straight Fort proved very partial. While this was also the day when the future champion Bula emerged, the opener set the flavour for the rest of the afternoon, which brought two further Irish-trained winners, Ballywilliam Boy in a division of the Gloucestershire Hurdle and Proud Tarquin in the Totalisator Champion Novices' Chase. The latter race would have produced an Irish one-two-three had the talented mare Glencaraig Lady not crashed out at the last. As it was, the result completed a double for Dreaper – and for Taaffe, whose last Cheltenham Festival in the saddle this was destined to be. There was encouragement too for L'Escargot's connections, with King Vulgan – the horse that had beaten him the previous month at sodden Navan – staying on up the hill to claim second place. Day two was dominated, as expected, by Persian War completing a hat-trick of Champion Hurdle triumphs. But it also brought disappointment for Dreaper, whose efforts to win the Arkle Challenge Trophy were thwarted for a second year running. His warm favourite

East Bound could do no better than fifth, with L'Escargot's stable companion Trentina trailing in some way further back.

And so to Gold Cup day. After thirty-one four-year-olds had thundered around the new course, lured by the £7,413 first prize on offer in the Daily Express Triumph Hurdle, the main event set off exactly twelve minutes late at 3.52pm. The market had settled on Kinloch Brae (15/8) and Spanish Steps (9/4) as much the most likely winners. French Tan was rated best of the rest at 8/1. Titus Oates and Larbawn exchanged the leadership throughout the early stages, before the favourite took over at the twelfth. It was eight fences later, as the leaders picked up speed, that the race sprang dramatically into life. Approaching the third-last, Kinloch Brae in the Arkle colours was beginning to string them out. French Tan was keeping pace a couple of lengths back. L'Escargot, his sheepskin noseband prominent, had eased into third spot some three lengths behind French Tan and looked to have every chance of fulfilling Joan Moore's expectations. The other seven survivors, headed by Spanish Steps, were struggling to hang on to the Irish trio's heels. In the last few strides before the fence, as they sped past the white-walled farmhouse that then overlooked this part of the track, Pat Taaffe brought French Tan up much closer behind the leader's haunches. 'I tried to get Kinloch Brae off the bit,' he later recalled. Usually a flawless and highly efficient jumper, the favourite got in too close and came to grief a couple of strides past the fence beside a stationary grey and white Land Rover. 'His jumping was so brilliant, slick and fast,' his jockey Timmy Hyde says more than fifty years later. 'He got very close to the fence and didn't get high enough. He got a terrible fall. He was stunned. He was never the same after-wards, neither his zest nor his jumping.' Hyde says he does not think the mishap was anything to do with Taaffe. 'He was still half a length behind me taking off,' he recalls. Further back in the field, the weakening Titus Oates also exited the race at this obstacle, bringing down Herring Gull.

It was at this point that Carberry's tactical nous came deci-sively into play. Quickening down the hill, he had L'Escargot up within striking distance of French Tan within a few strides, breaking well clear of Spanish Steps in the process. Going over the last, the race was still in the balance between the two Irish contenders. French Tan jumped it better, but as they climbed towards the line L'Escargot's much-questioned stamina came into its own. With Carberry driving for all he was worth, the lithe chestnut began inching ahead. As they passed the winning-post, the margin was one and a half lengths. The duel had carried them a good ten lengths clear of the top English horse, Spanish Steps.

The winning jockey was notably understated as he savoured the unexpected victory. 'All three of us were just coasting in front when Kinloch Brae fell,' he observed. 'Mine wasn't jumping brilliantly – just fiddling his fences nicely.' With victory attained, Dan Moore acknowledged that, given a free hand, he would have targeted a different race. 'I thought 2½ miles was his best trip,' he said. 'I wanted to run him in the Two-Mile Champion Chase, but Mr Guest was particu-larly anxious to go for the Gold Cup.' For his part, L'Escargot's owner was happy to admit the gelding had outperformed expectations. 'I didn't think there was a horse in the world to beat Kinloch Brae,' he exclaimed. It was also an excellent result for the Hobday: French Tan, like the winner, had undergone the surgical procedure. Taaffe and Dreaper did finally secure their third winner of the festival when L'Escargot's oldest rival, Garrynagree, secured a comfortable victory in the Cathcart Challenge Cup, emulating Kinloch Brae who had strolled home in 1969.

Little more than three years after his first race, L'Escargot was now suddenly one of the best-known horses in the business. After a well-earned rest, he would be dispatched back across the Atlantic to try his luck in yet another new event – the richly endowed Colonial Cup.

Chapter 14

A rival for the Grand National

In a time of ambitious new jump-racing initiatives, the Colonial Cup stands out as the most ambitious of all. The idea – already in train when L'Escargot pulled off his Cheltenham Gold Cup upset – was to attract the cream of international steeplechasers to take on the best American horses in an annual event at an established track in South Carolina. An early mention of the project, published in *The New York Times* in February 1970, maintained that the new race 'could challenge England's Grand National as the world's premier event in a few years' – though it should be added that this was a period of lingering uncertainty over the Aintree marathon's long-term future. Later, in July, South Carolina's governor, Robert McNair, who was acting as honorary chairman of the event's executive commit-tee, invited Queen Elizabeth the Queen Mother to enter a horse and present a trophy to the winner. It was reported subsequently that she sent a representative to the race, Viscount Cobham.*

The proposed venue was certainly worthy of such an occasion, even if the obstacles and, as it turned out, the going might strike the European contingent as a little out of the ordinary. Springdale racecourse in Camden, about 30 miles north-east of the state capital Columbia, was so spacious that the entire proposed 2mi 6½f event could be accommodated with no fence jumped more than once. It was in racing country, with the first formal meeting in the town predating the Battle of Trafalgar by three years. And it was well used to staging a big annual event in the shape of the Carolina Cup, a highlight of the regional social calendar, which had originated at Springdale in 1930. At the time of the inaugural running of the new race, the so-called Camden Training Center encompassed more than a thousand acres, with stabling and training facilities for 285 horses. A winding path through pine-scented woodland connected Springdale to a training ground for flat horses called Wrenfield Track. The geographic location meant that winters ended earlier in Camden than other leading US jump-racing hotspots. And with the appeal of steeplechasing dwindling in the urban centres where it had established a foothold fifty or sixty years earlier, it was hoped that introduction of a prestigious

---

* A telegram dispatched from Buckingham Palace to 'The Colonial Cup Committee' ahead of the 1971 race read: 'I send you my warmest good wishes on the occasion of the second running of the Colonial Cup. I hope it will be an outstanding success and I only am sorry that I have no horse suitable for the race. Elizabeth R Queen Mother.'

new fixture would provide a focal point around which the sport could rally.

To stand even the slightest chance of getting off the ground, of course, a venture of this magnitude was going to require copious amounts of one particular commodity: money. Fortunately, the training centre was owned by a grey-eyed gunpowder heiress called Marion duPont Scott. Horses had been one of the out-and-out passions of duPont Scott's immensely privileged life. While the great and the good of North American steeplechasing – including L'Escargot's owner Raymond Guest, who sat alongside duPont Scott and banking dynast Paul Mellon on the Colonial Cup executive committee – could be relied upon to do their bit, duPont Scott, in her mid-seventies, was wealthy and committed enough to act as a sort of guarantor of last resort, should that be necessary.*

At the instigation of duPont Scott and her right-hand man Raymond Woolfe, two lures were placed to ensure that this inaugural Colonial Cup would entice an international field of the requisite high calibre. First, the purse would be set at an eye-popping $100,000 – about twice the size of the Temple Gwathmey and more than any other steeplechase bar the Grand Steeple-Chase de Paris. Second, as Wesley Faulkenberry, registrar of the Camden-based National Steeplechase Museum, told me, duPont Scott would personally pay all expenses incurred by non-USA-based runners and

---

* DuPont Scott's main home was at Montpelier in Virginia. However, she also owned a property in Camden, where the DuPont de Nemours company, having diversified from explosives, opened an acrylic fibre plant in 1950.

their immediate entourage in bringing them to Springdale in time for the appointed date – 14 November 1970.

Foreign nominations for the new race, which would form part of South Carolina's tricentennial celebration, closed in early August, having attracted more than forty horses from ten countries. At this stage, France was the best-represented nation, with nine nominees. The Irish contingent of seven was of the highest-possible quality. American owners, meanwhile, were said to have nominated as many as 150 possible entrants. The English trainer Fred Rimell's nominations caught the eye of many knowledgeable observers since they were hurdlers not steeplechasers. This encouraged the notion that, with its speed and relatively soft brush obstacles, American chasing should be viewed as an intermediate form of the sport, pitched somewhere between stamina-sapping, European-style chasing and traditional hurdling. Photographs of the inaugural race confirm that the obstacles used, at 56 inches, were similar in size and appearance to European steeplechase fences but for the aprons, which were fashioned from horizontally laid branches. European participants, though, observed that they were significantly softer than the fences encountered routinely at home.

The executive committee gave itself the best part of a month to decide which would-be runners to extend all-expenses-paid invitations to. It was emphasised that those not picked could come and race nevertheless. They would have to pay their way but would not face nomination or starting fees. By September, it looked like all three of the Ireland-based horses that had led the way approaching the third-last fence in the Cheltenham Gold Cup six months earlier would make the trip. In the end, Kinloch Brae dropped out, but French Tan duly joined L'Escargot on the Springdale starting line along with Herring Gull.

It had been made clear from the moment the Ballysax gelding won that reputation-making duel up the Prestbury Park slope that the Colonial Cup would be a major target. This left Dan Moore with the conundrum of how best to get the horse race-fit a few weeks earlier than usual, in a way that would not risk leaving him jaded at the very moment when he needed to be back at concert pitch. With steeplechasing's future ever more under the microscope at Aqueduct and Belmont Park,* the solution presented itself closer to home. L'Escargot would tune up with a spot of early-autumn flat-racing at his local track, The Curragh. This might have the added benefit of preparing him, once again, for the faster pace of racing on the western side of the Atlantic. If it occurred to the trainer that steering clear of early-season jump races should also minimise any prospect of injury in the run-up to the chestnut's attempt to secure another big purse for connections, however, he was in for an unsettling surprise.

On 26 September, L'Escargot was entered in the October Stakes over 12 furlongs. He ended up being withdrawn at the start. This was after sustaining a kick from another runner, which left him with a cut high up on one leg. The *Irish Times* reported that it 'must be touch and go whether

---

* After significant changes in the 1971 season, jump-racing was finally evicted from the two New York venues following a decision by the board of trustees of the New York Racing Association in November 1971.

he will be fit enough to contest' the Colonial Cup, although any such suggestion was quickly scotched by Moore, who pronounced the injuries 'not serious' while revealing that he intended to give the horse two further flat runs before departure for Carolina. He was as good as his word. First, on 17 October – the day the great Nijinsky was beaten in his last race at Newmarket – L'Escargot ran in his second Irish Cesarewitch, finishing eighteenth out of twenty-four. Two weeks later, he carried top weight, albeit only 9st 3lb, in a shorter race, the 1½-mile Crotanstown Handicap Stakes. He was not without his supporters, being sent off as joint fifth-favourite, but once again finished well down another big field of twenty-three. It was just over a week after this uneventful outing that the gelding set off on the third North American odyssey of his singular career.

Arthur Moore remembers European participants in the race congregating in Shannon before boarding a 'propeller job' initially to Halifax, Nova Scotia. 'It took about eight hours,' he says. Facilities for the horses were 'just the same as though we were flying to Cheltenham. They had their stalls. They were elite horses; they were good travellers.' One further detail from this Canadian stopover has stayed with Moore for over fifty years. 'It was about half a mile from the plane to the hangar,' he tells me. 'We went in to have a drink and for a rest. I ordered a Winter's Tale sherry.' To which the response was: 'What age are you, boy?' Moore answered the question: he was over the legal drinking age. Reply: 'I want to see your passport.' As a result, Moore had to make a lengthy round trip to fetch the document. Upon his return he discovered that one of the locals had kindly bought him his drink. 'He thought I deserved it after that.'

As well as the Irish trio, Young Ash Leaf had travelled from Ken Oliver's Scottish stable, with Big Valley making the trip from Toby Balding's yard in southern England.* A horse called Sacramento represented Switzerland, with Niksu and Ermitage flying the flag for France. The great Crisp had already been on site for some days, having made the long trek from Australia. 'Crisp came back with us,' Moore recalls. 'He was a gorgeous big horse.'† Fred Winter, the English trainer who took him on, reacted in much the same way when Crisp arrived in Lambourn, remarking, 'Just look at the depth of his chest: he must have a big heart in there.' For all that, the horse's globetrotting had taken its toll on his condition. Nor had he previously experienced the rigours of a northern-hemisphere winter. Jockey Richard Pitman recalled that his coat 'grew to almost unknown lengths within a fortnight, making him look like a hairy hat-rack'.

Among the US contingent that still made up the bulk of the field, Top Bid, trained by the Moores' relative Mikey Smithwick, was viewed as the likeliest winner, having won that season's edition of the Temple Gwathmey. The Moores might also have recognised the name High Patches, winner of the American Grand National that L'Escargot had been

---

* Balding's father and uncles had been well-known polo players in the USA. One uncle had a home in Camden.

† Nicknamed the Black Kangaroo, Crisp's most famous race came in the 1973 Grand National, which he led throughout, only to be caught on the line by Red Rum.

expected to contest the previous year. The race's international prestige was further augmented by the presence of Michael O'Hehir, the well-known Irish commentator. Radio Éireann broadcast O'Hehir's race commentary commencing at 9.50pm Irish time.

It is tempting to speculate as to Dan Moore's reaction on first setting eye on the twenty-page race programme. Its cover star was none other than Battleship, the little chestnut stallion who had so narrowly – and agonisingly – deprived him of what would have been his greatest victory as a jockey in the 1938 Grand National at Aintree. Battleship had belonged to Marion duPont Scott, who had been in the stands at Liverpool that changeable late-March afternoon more than three decades earlier. The image – a reproduction of a portrait set at Montpelier by the artist William Smithson Broadhead – would have reminded Moore and Raymond Guest alike that the Grand National was a prize that, for all their efforts, continued to elude them both.

It had been hoped that a crowd of around 30,000 would be attracted by the inaugural Colonial Cup event. The organisers were unlucky, however. Dawn on race day broke on a heavy early-morning mist and, as time passed, intermittent showers turned into steady rain that set in about half an hour before the off. The event was still a big draw – local traffic was heavy, motels full and rental cars taken – but attendance was reckoned to be more like 20,000 than 30,000. Among these, as *The New York Times* commented, were 'the real "blue bloods" of the sport – the Whittakers, the Phippses, the Wideners, the duPonts, the Mellons, the Guests and the Firestones'. Elizabeth Whitney, the paper reported, had 'tried to beat the jam by requesting to land a helicopter in the infield', but, alas, 'her request was turned down'. L'Escargot's owner tracked his gelding's progress from the stand in a check flat cap, wielding field glasses.

The contest was not an especially happy experience for the European raiders. Indeed, Herring Gull, after crossing an ocean to get there, ran out before the first of eighteen fences. For a while, Crisp and Young Ash Leaf shared pace-making duties with a US horse called Peach II, but both had dropped back well before Shadow Brook made the first serious move. At the penultimate obstacle another American challenger, Jaunty, hit the front. These two still led the way over the last, but the writing – in the shape of the fast-finishing Top Bid – was on the wall. Streaking to the front with a perfectly timed run under jockey Joe Aitcheson Jnr, Mrs Ogden Phipps's six-year-old crossed the line with a one-and-a-half-length advantage. Having been nursed quietly along by Tommy Carberry into a position where he could conceivably have launched a challenge against less fleet-footed adversaries, L'Escargot finished far from disgraced in fourth place. He might have made the frame had he not suffered interference when Wustenchef, the only faller, came down. Fourth was good enough to secure a $5,000 payday for his owner. By comparison, Crisp finished sixth, French Tan and Pat Taaffe were thirteenth, and Big Valley and Eddie Harty sixteenth.

Half a century on, Arthur Moore most remembers how hard the ground was. He says that L'Escargot 'ran a blinder'. By this token, it may have been a pity, from a European perspective, that the rain did not set in earlier. Immediately after the race, Taaffe's chief preoccupation was the softness of the fences. 'The pace was really fast for my fellow,' he said. 'It killed his chance completely. It is because the fences are so soft that the pace is so intense.' Harty, though, was most impressed by the quality of the Springdale course, arguing that the track was 'good enough for our Grand National', which he had won on Highland Wedding just a year and a half before. He went on: 'If Aintree is ever closed, this would be a perfect home for the Grand National', but 'if we are to have steeplechasing on an international level, the authorities will have to adopt a stand-ard type of fence, which is the crux all the time.'

As it turned out, the Colonial Cup survived all the way through until 2016. This was even though, in Faulkenberry's words, 'the race meet never made money and suffered from poor attendance its whole life'. That inaugural contest was staged on the same weekend as a big college football game in Columbia between South Carolina and Duke. This seems to have been a recurrent issue. According to Faulkenberry, the race 'was never embraced by the local college and university students in the way the Carolina Cup was, due to competing with American Football for their attendance'. For all that, the Cup has left a legacy of substantial good-will. 'It was a deeply beloved event by the people in Camden,' Faulkenberry explains. 'It was what the town was known for internationally. The most-asked question I get from visitors to the museum is "What happened to the Colonial Cup?" or "When is the Colonial Cup going to come back?" In terms of finances, it is hard to find any reason to claim the Colonial Cup as anything but a failure. Conversely, in terms of culture, impact and legacy, it is difficult to qualify it as anything other than a success.'

That you needed an exceptional horse to win the race was underlined over the next few years. The next two victors – Inkslinger, another Smithwick-trained chaser that won, ridden by Carberry, in 1971, and Soothsayer – would go on to become Cheltenham festival winners, the former for Dan Moore.

Having been reacquainted with both flat-racing and American-style steeplechasing over the course of an eventful autumn, Guest's versatile gelding would be asked to go hurdling for his next public outing. Guest himself was reshuffling his horseracing interests one more time. Entering his sixty-fourth year, and with his diplomatic duties long behind him, he had decided to cut back his holdings in Ireland.

Chapter 15

Down in the mud

The sales agent must have been thrilled with the headline. "'The Stud Farm That Has Everything" Goes On Market,' announced the article by the *Irish Field*'s property correspondent. The property in question was Raymond Guest's Ballygoran Stud in County Kildare and the report signalled that, more than two years after his spell as US ambassador to Ireland had come to an end, Guest was winding down his Irish breeding operation. With publicity like that, it was not very long before a deal was sealed. In the very first days of 1971, it emerged that the 335-acre farm with its immaculate six-bedroom Georgian residence and a main stud incorporating forty-four boxes would pass into the hands of Redmond Gallagher. The purchaser was a one-time motor-racing enthusiast and a member of the Urney chocolate family. The selling price was put at £419,000.

Guest had pumped no end of investment into the property during more than seven years of ownership. But his first Derby winner, Larkspur, had been shipped to Japan some years earlier and his second, the peerless Sir Ivor, had recently departed for

Kentucky, whence he had come.* The ex-ambassador would not be cutting ties with Ireland altogether but, having moved back to Virginia, it probably made sense to concentrate his bloodstock interests there.

A farewell party for Sir Ivor had been held in July, at the end of his two breeding seasons at Ballygoran. Invitees reported that the US-bound stallion, whose stud fee – latterly 8,000 guineas – was thought to have been the highest in Europe, was full of high spirits. Guests were treated to barbecued steaks served in a marquee, and John Moore, Guest's successor as US ambassador, gave a well-received speech. The horse set out for his new home in Bluegrass country that very evening.

While Ballygoran was up for sale, L'Escargot had returned safely from South Carolina and was once again on the list of entries for the Irish Sweeps Hurdle. This time he would stand his ground. With £12,500 added, the winner's purse would be the richest prize ever offered for a hurdle race in Ireland or Great Britain. With that sort of money on the line, a top-quality field for the contest, set for Fairyhouse on 28 December, was confidently expected.

The biggest name of all in hurdling at this time was still Persian War. But the three-time champion had undergone a soft palate operation since his latest Cheltenham festival win in March. This had sparked noisy debate over whether the doughty campaigner could regain former heights. It was this debate that dominated the build-up to the big race. Larry

---

* Sir Ivor – widely credited with putting the Keeneland sales on the international bloodstock map – would stand for many years at the Claiborne Farm base of Bull Hancock, the man who had bought him for Guest as a yearling in 1966.

Lynx in *The People* described the Fairyhouse event – under the headline, 'War On Ireland!' – as 'the make-or-break test for Persian War'. He argued that the tongue-strapped superstar 'MUST win to silence the critics who insist he's no longer the horse he was'. The horse, which had a new trainer in Arthur Pitt, had travelled to Ireland well ahead of the race. He was being lodged at Charlie Weld's stables on The Curragh where he was guarded, as Lynx put it, 'like the crown jewels'. Media interest in his every movement and in comments made by Henry Alper, his talkative owner, was intense.

Not for the first time the yuletide racing programme was decimated by bad weather. On the day of the Irish Sweeps Hurdle, five meetings were snowed off in England. Fairyhouse survived, but conditions were absolutely terrible. The afternoon brought sleet, snow, hail and rain. One correspondent wrote feelingly of how a 'sleet-laced wind straight from Siberia blew across the plains of Meath right up into the Fairyhouse stands'. Worse still: 'Frequent showers of hail pelted our faces like gunshot.'

Nine other runners joined Persian War and L'Escargot on the starting line. At least three of these were seen as plausible winners: Caro Bello, based in Ireland and thought to be returning to his best; and the English pair Hunter's Treasure, a filly with a seven-win streak among her accomplishments, and the very promising Inishmaan. In the end, though, punters settled on L'Escargot as the most likely challenger to Persian War, who was sent off as 5/4 favourite. Their money brought the versatile gelding's starting price down to 4/1. Perhaps some of these gamblers remembered his impressive victory in the Scalp Hurdle nearly two years before, gained in similarly atrocious conditions. This was not to be one of the

Moore representative's better performances, however. After Hunter's Treasure and another veteran of the trek to South Carolina, Herring Gull, had led in the early stages, Persian War and Jimmy Uttley hit the front at halfway and were never headed. The final margin was described by one reporter as 'a contemptuous eight lengths'. Tommy Carberry and L'Escargot tried initially to stay within striking distance of the champion, only to tire and trail in an 'exhausted' fourth.

While some might have blamed the lacklustre run on fatigue in the wake of the horse's latest transatlantic expedition, Arthur Moore is inclined to attribute it to the tactics followed. 'I reckon that Tommy kicked on too soon that day,' he tells me. As it was, the great hurdler had come through his 'make-or-break test' with flying colours. It turned out to be something of a last hurrah, though: this dominant slog through the Fairyhouse mire was the final major win of his magnificent career.

Another big story broke on that wintry Meath afternoon: Pat Taaffe, perennial partner of the great Arkle, announced his retirement from the saddle at the age of forty. His very last ride came in the race that followed the Irish Sweeps Hurdle, the 3-mile Christmas Handicap Chase, aboard the more-than-useful Proud Tarquin. But of all sports disciplines, steeplechasing is among the most grudging in its apportionment of fairy-tale endings. Taaffe landed one final time down in the mud adjacent to the drumming hooves of the other runners, after taking a fall when leading at the sixth fence from home. The race was won with utmost ease by Cnoc Dubh. Arthur Moore was well placed to assess the calibre of the performance, trailing in second on King's Sprite fifteen lengths in arrears.

Proud Tarquin was there again twelve days later at Punchestown, where L'Escargot raced over European-style steeplechase fences for the first time since winning the sport's blue-riband event for chasers, the Cheltenham Gold Cup, nearly ten months previously. It was to prove a landmark afternoon for the now eight-year-old chestnut gelding, but not in the way his handlers would have wanted.

The field for the Rathside Chase, over 3 miles, was small but perfectly formed. Raymond Guest's horse would be top weight, but he would not be the only 1970 Cheltenham festival winner to line up. Proud Tarquin's stable companion Straight Fort – good enough to edge out Royal Relief in the Two-Mile Champion Chase – would be there too. So would No Other, a horse that had run against Proud Tarquin five times in little more than a year, with honours about even. King's Sprite and Arthur Moore would be the outsiders of the six. Most intriguingly of all, French Tan, runner-up in the Gold Cup and a fellow traveller with L'Escargot on that trail-blazing Colonial Cup expedition, would be on the starting line and in receipt of 4lb from his Ballysax-based rival. Pat Taaffe, plainly, would not be there. As a result, French Tan would be ridden by Bill McLernon, a talented amateur jockey, and Proud Tarquin by Peter McLoughlin, a member of Tom Dreaper's loyal and knowledgeable team. Conditions were a sight better than at Fairyhouse but still wind-blown and with the going soft.

Proud Tarquin and No Other bounded away from the flag-fall and took up a clear lead until No Other almost came down at the second obstacle. This enabled French Tan and L'Escargot to take closer order. At around 2 miles, Proud Tarquin was caught and the six runners, all still standing, bunched up. French Tan hit the front before the third-last fence and looked stronger and stronger, pulling clear of Proud Tarquin and L'Escargot, who were engaged in what looked like their own private battle for the runner-up spot. But jockey Bobby Coonan was conjuring a finish from No Other, and the pair shot through into second place before the last, in vain pursuit of the runaway leader. This final fence was then hit by L'Escargot with such force as to unship Carberry, who came crashing to ground as McLoughlin, just a stride or two further on, glanced over his shoulder in his orange-and-white-quartered cap.

In twenty-nine races across three countries, it was the first time that the Moores' star performer had failed to complete the course. It was not a big thing in itself, perhaps. This was jump-racing: accidents happened; you learnt to expect the unexpected. But having now endured a five-race losing streak, the longest of his career – albeit in an extremely diverse sequence of races, some of which he had no prospect of winning – well, was the habit setting in? Had the sheer variety of the tasks set before the horse triggered a loss of confidence? Had his unusually extensive travel itinerary worn him down – and out? At this point these were no more than questions, prompted in part by the contrast with the apparent smoothness of French Tan's tuning-up campaign. An answer of sorts appeared later in January, when it was reported that L'Escargot had cut his leg in the Irish Sweeps Hurdle and so had not been at his absolute best at Punchestown.

There was no doubt, though, that the spotlight would be on Guest's gelding like never before in the final weeks of his Cheltenham preparations.

Chapter 16

The new Leopardstown

Irish jump-racing had never seen anything quite like it. When Leopardstown racecourse's new million-pound development was opened to the public in January 1971, it was as if the sport had been ushered brusquely into the modern age – and then some. A new four-storey stand, accounting for the bulk of the investment, introduced creature comforts the like of which winter racegoers on the island had simply not known before. There were restaurants, bars, a children's playground (with attendants), a bank, a VIP floor, closed-circuit television with 'a profusion of sets', escalators that operated on what one writer described as 'a tidal flow basis' and – perhaps most welcome of all – there was central heating. As one visitor eulogised, 'Gone are those grim winter evenings spent muffled in the very bowels of swaddling suede coats or huddled (one entire racing congregation at a time) around a solitary brazier in a wind-blasted enclosure.' Such scenes had been consigned to history in Foxrock by '£5,000 worth of boilers' along with storage space for a reassuringly copious 9 tons of fuel. The money had not been spent exclusively with the well-being of racecourse patrons in mind. Behind the project was a hard-nosed plan to apply modern management methods to the venue, creating a more family-friendly environment with a view to maximising use of the facilities far beyond race-days. Management spoke in terms of forty days of racing and 300 days of usage per year.

Reopening day on 13 January could have been handled better. A tide of curious Dubliners descended on the place, resulting in many of the amenities getting swamped. But the occasion enabled improvements to the actual course to be fully appreciated for the first time. These involved most notably a widening of the running track by 200ft to permit more frequent switches to unused ground when the racing surface got churned up, and a re-siting of the water-jump to a more prominent position. The new obstacle was said by the *Irish Times* to be 'the cynosure of all eyes' during this inaugural January meeting.

This 'new' Leopardstown would be the impressive backdrop for L'Escargot's final warm-up race for Cheltenham on 20 February. His trainer Dan Moore had opted for the same staging-post as the previous year – the Leopardstown Chase; after all, it had worked well enough last time. But, of course, this year there would be no need to run the race at Navan.

A strong field of ten, including the 1970 winner King Vulgan, would go to post, but pre-race chatter was monopolised by one horse: Glencaraig Lady. The Francis Flood-trained mare had emerged as a live contender in what looked to be another wide-open Cheltenham Gold Cup by beating Even Keel over 3 miles at Ascot. Just how highly she was being talked of is underlined by the *Daily Mirror*'s coverage on the morning of the Leopardstown race. 'Arkle twice won the Leopardstown Chase carrying 12st 7lb,' recalled journalist Tony Sweeney. 'But even if the champion was in today's line-up I believe he would have found a tough fight on his hands in attempting the concession of a stone to Glencaraig Lady.' Given that L'Escargot, quite apart from showing less than sparkling form, was being asked to give 9lb to the new pretender, it was little surprise that she was seen almost universally as the one to beat. She was duly sent off as the odds-on favourite.

As the countdown to Cheltenham ticked remorselessly on, it seemed this was one of those years when some of the main contenders' fortunes would swing violently this way and that – to the despair of ante-post punters. This had already been demonstrated in a three-horse race on 5 February at Sandown Park in one of the leafier London suburbs. All three starters in the Gainsborough Chase had run in L'Escargot's Gold Cup the previous March and all three were expected to take him on again this time around, with two of them among the favourites. There was the giant The Dikler, with a year's extra jumping experience and undiminished power; there was French Tan, such an impressive winner at Punchestown; and there was Titus Oates, a Gold Cup faller in 1970 and an outsider eleven months on. And yet victory at Sandown went to Titus Oates, triggering an abrupt reassessment of the Gold Cup market. Worse was to follow for supporters of French Tan. The 1970 Gold Cup runner-up was found to be lame in the wake of his two-and-a-half-length defeat. Having started February as a horse deemed well capable of turning the tables on Raymond Guest's gelding in the 1971 Gold Cup renewal, he ended it as a confirmed non-runner.

At new Leopardstown, in ground too soft for either of their liking, neither of the big guns mounted a serious challenge, yet at the end of the 3 miles, their respective Gold Cup prospects had been comprehensively re-evaluated. L'Escargot, though not at his smoothest, had appeared to knuckle down and grow into the race. He finished third nine lengths behind the winner. The *Irish Times* man observed that the gelding was 'a bit slow at some of his fences, but he certainly began to pick them up in the closing stages'. Trainer Dan Moore's cautiously upbeat verdict was that he 'ran much better than I thought he might in that ground.' Glencaraig Lady could do no better than fifth, a discouraging outcome since the rematch at Cheltenham would be at level weights. Rather like Moore, Flood observed it was 'not her ground'. Furthermore, 'she did make a few mistakes' and 'being away from a racecourse for two months did not help'. One observer had the fleeting impression as they entered the final bend that the favourite was 'about to come through and win'. In fact, 'she was very, very tired when hitting the last fence hard'. It was noted a few days later that she had sustained a 'slight rap on a joint' in running.

One of the lightweights at the head of proceedings in the final stages was none other than Arthur Moore, aboard his regular partner, King's Sprite. They were receiving a massive 33lb from Tommy Carberry and L'Escargot. Macroney, the 16/1 shot with whom he was vying for this high-profile victory in front of a big and animated crowd, was receiving 4lb more. Moore remembers seeing jockey Paddy Kiely ahead of him and

Jimmy Brogan, who bought the young L'Escargot but died before his racing debut. (Courtesy of Pamela Morton)

L'Escargot (on left, jumping) was a good enough hurdler to win at Cheltenham, though he proved no match for the mighty Persian War (second from right) in the 1969 Champion Hurdle. (© PA Images / Alamy)

Dan Moore's wife, Joan, established a close bond with the horse.
(Courtesy of Arthur Moore)

L'Escargot's owner Raymond Guest enjoyed great success on the flat. When his colt, Sir Ivor, won the 1968 Derby ridden by Lester Piggott, however, ambassadorial duties kept Guest away. Here, his wife, Caroline Murat, leads horse and jockey in after their success. (© PA Images / Alamy)

L'Escargot (left) won his first Cheltenham Gold Cup in 1970 as a 33/1 outsider. After clearing the last alongside Pat Taaffe's mount French Tan (right), he powered away to score by a length and a half. (© PA Images / Alamy)

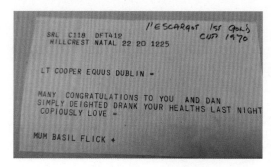

A telegram sent to Tom Cooper, who had bought L'Escargot on Raymond Guest's behalf, after the gelding's 1970 Cheltenham Gold Cup victory.

(Courtesy of Valerie Cooper)

The field for the inaugural Colonial Cup, run in South Carolina and offering a $100,000 purse, was exceptionally strong.

(Courtesy of The Carolina Cup Racing Association and the National Steeplechase Museum)

A portrait of Battleship, the horse that had narrowly thwarted Dan Moore's Grand National ambitions as a jockey thirty-two years earlier, adorned the cover of the first Colonial Cup programme.

(Courtesy of The Carolina Cup Racing Association and the National Steeplechase Museum)

The grey, Flying Wild (centre), was one of several horses to carry the Guest colours at Aintree unsuccessfully before L'Escargot's fourth and final Grand National attempt(© Smith Archive / Alamy)

Red Rum's trainer Donald 'Ginger' McCain celebrates with a pint after the horse's first Grand National win in 1973. (© Trinity Mirror / Mirrorpix / Alamy)

Jockey Richard Pitman, twice a Grand National runner-up, reading about L'Escargot's prospects while shedding pounds in a Turkish bath.
(© cranhamphoto.com)

L'Escargot's regular jockey Tommy Carberry pictured with Raymond Guest's daughter Virginia, who gave him a snail's shell for good luck ahead of the 1975 Grand National.
(© cranhamphoto.com)

Thirty-one horses and jockeys lined up for L'Escargot's fourth attempt to win the Grand National in 1975.
(© cranhamphoto.com)

The 1975 Grand National was the tenth and last time L'Escargot raced against the gutsy Spanish Steps, whose jockey Bill Smith (far left) was convinced he was going to win.
(© PA Images / Alamy)

They're off in the 1975 Grand National! L'Escargot (blinkered, number 4) is already on the heels of the early leaders. (© cranhamphoto.com)

L'Escargot and Carberry soar over The Chair. Disaster had nearly struck just a couple of minutes earlier at the much smaller seventh fence.
(© cranhamphoto.com)

Red Rum and Brian Fletcher lead L'Escargot over the last en route to their second Grand National victory in 1974… (© Keystone Press / Alamy)

…Twelve months later at the same fence, Carberry and L'Escargot have seized the upper hand prior to galloping away to win by fifteen lengths. (© cranhamphoto.com)

SNAIL'S PACE IS A CRACKER!

Brilliant Carberry helps to end Red Rum series

L'Escargot breaks Irish losing run at Aintree

CHAMPAGNE TREAT FOR L'ESCARGOT

THE SUNDAY TELEGRAPH   APRIL 6, 1975

Sweet revenge for L'Escargot

Snail's pace at last for L'Escargot

Headlines from Arthur Moore's scrapbook hail L'Escargot's fourth-time-lucky Grand National triumph. (Courtesy of Arthur Moore)

A delighted Raymond Guest (left) leads in L'Escargot, having finally fulfilled a lifetime dream. Trainer Dan Moore (right) also savours the victory, thirty-seven years after his own Grand National heartbreak. (© cranhamphoto.com)

observing that Macroney 'kept jumping to the right'. After clearing the penultimate fence, Moore and King's Sprite 'slipped up his inside'. By his own admission, Moore had 'hit the front too soon', however. Macroney came back on the run-in to win by six lengths. It transpired that the result had a very considerable silver lining for the runner-up: had he won, King's Sprite would have been burdened with an extra weight penalty when he lined up for the Irish Grand National nearly two months later.

This was also the day and the place where jockey Bobby Beasley – whose career had succumbed to the after-effects of heavy falls allied with weight problems and alcoholism – achieved the first win of his remarkable comeback. In the opening race on the card, a twenty-eight-runner cavalry charge called the Stillorgan Maiden Hurdle, the popular veteran drove Norwegian Flag to victory by three-quarters of a length, earning a tumultuous reception.* The rider later described the triumph, and the manner of its attainment, as 'the psychological boost that I had needed'. As he also said: 'The old Beasley was back.'

While most people in Britain and Ireland were grappling with the challenge of the new decimal coinage, introduced on 15 February, Raymond Guest was resuming his assault on the Aintree Grand National. Rather than dispatch L'Escargot on this forlorn quest, however, he opted once again to dust off his cheque-book. In early February it emerged that the American had bought Cnoc Dubh, the horse that had won Pat Taaffe's sleet-drenched last race so impressively from King's Sprite and

---

* Both Norwegian Flag and Lockyersleigh – the winner of the second race, the Scalp Hurdle – were the offspring of L'Escargot's deceased sire, Escart III. It was a reminder of how deep an imprint the French-bred stallion might have left on jump-racing in the British Isles had he lived.

Arthur Moore. The new acquisition had already been welcomed at Ballysax after travelling up from his previous base in County Kilkenny. Before the end of the month, Guest had splurged again, this time on Smooth Dealer, winner of the previous year's Thyestes Chase, an accepted proving-ground for stayers run at Gowran Park. Like his new stablemate, Smooth Dealer would act on soft ground, of which there had been no shortage that winter, and was endowed with stamina in abundance.

As March beckoned, the ever-shifting pre-festival betting market had installed L'Escargot as Gold Cup favourite. Yet it was still advisable to pay close attention. Five days after the reigning champion's highly satisfactory Leopardstown run-out, Kinloch Brae made a winning return at Wincanton after a long spell on the sidelines, only to break down in the process. This appeared to put paid to his chances just as they were being revived. And then, with just a few days to go before the race, came the most unexpected twist of all: Spanish Steps, third behind L'Escargot and French Tan the previous year, would be absent from the 1971 Gold Cup owing to a mix-up over declarations.

One thing was clear: in contrast to 1970, L'Escargot would not be able to fly in under the Prestbury Park radar. This time a lot more Irish money would be riding on his shoulders. The pressure was on. As a precaution, Arthur Moore bedded down for the last week before the Ballysax team's departure for Gloucestershire in a caravan outside the chestnut gelding's stable. In a Proustian flashback, he told one interviewer he can still smell the gas from the burner he used to heat up his hot chocolate. It would be a small price to pay if L'Escargot could etch his name into sporting history as a repeat Gold Cup winner.

Chapter 17

Illustrious company

If the vicissitudes of jump-racing had not already done enough to mar the 1971 Cheltenham Gold Cup as a spectacle, the unreliable West Country weather gods completed the job. Fifteen hours of continuous rainfall leading up to the final-day festival programme left the course saturated. Conditions were difficult enough for the race's planned starting position to be relocated and a fence omitted. One English hope, Titus Oates, was declared a non-runner, joining French Tan, Kinloch Brae and Spanish Steps on the sidelines. Another, Into View,* saddled by in-form Lambourn trainer Fred Winter, disliked the going so much his challenge was effectively blunted.

This did not prevent Paul Kelleway's mount from setting off as joint favourite of three along with L'Escargot and another talented young Irish horse called Leap Frog. The latest in a long list of fine chasers to emerge from Tom Dreaper's yard

---

* Into View, a Vulgan foal, had finished fifth in the 1969 Champion Hurdle when L'Escargot came sixth.

north of Dublin, Leap Frog had won three of his four races in the 1970–71 season. These included the second running of the Wills Premier Chase, the innovative new Haydock event whose inaugural edition L'Escargot had claimed two months before battling to victory in the 1970 Gold Cup. The only horse to have beaten Leap Frog so far, as the season approached its finale, was Into View in a 2-mile chase at Ascot. While some wondered whether the seven-year-old would have benefited from another race pre-Cheltenham, Tom Dreaper's son Jim argued that he performed best when fresh. 'If Leap Frog is kept working all the time he trains off,' Dreaper asserted. 'He had a good rest before the Wills and this worked. He now has a rest before Cheltenham.' The Dreapers were well known for espousing a 'less is more' philosophy with the horses in their care – and, with Tom Dreaper's record, who was to argue? Of the other runners in the small field of eight that had defied the slings and arrows of what seemed like particularly outrageous fortune that year and made it to the starting line, Glencaraig Lady and The Dikler were seen as possible contenders if events went their way.

With conditions dictating a steady pace, there was at first little to distract the bedraggled crowd from the dampness of their situation. Royal Toss, the Welsh Grand National winner, led the way. Leap Frog dropped back to the rear following an early error. The Dreaper horse began to make up ground on the second circuit, however, with Glencaraig Lady now in front. As the strung-out field approached the third-last, Leap Frog had worked his way back to third position and – with L'Escargot lying second, in spite of a tendency to hang right when he jumped – the Irish contingent already looked to have the race within their grasp. It was at this point, for the second year running, that the race dramatically changed complexion. Glencaraig Lady cleared the obstacle but knuckled over on landing. This left Tommy Carberry and L'Escargot in the lead, though with Leap Frog and Val O'Brien close enough to entertain ambitions of mounting a challenge, especially given the new leader's jumping issues. For a few moments, as Raymond Guest's horse slowed and again veered right approaching the last, O'Brien's white cap loomed up menacingly on the inner. There was nothing wrong with L'Escargot's engine, however. Having clambered over the fence, he ran on much the stronger up the punishing Prestbury Park hill to score by a convincing ten lengths.

If the race itself had been far from a classic, the outcome elevated L'Escargot's name into some seriously illustrious company. As more than one correspondent trumpeted, he had become the fifth horse to win the Cheltenham Gold Cup in successive years. The other four: Easter Hero, Golden Miller, Cottage Rake and Arkle.

Would he have beaten Glencaraig Lady had the mare stayed upright? It is impossible to say. Carberry told reporters he thought he had the race 'in the bag'. But Glencaraig Lady's jockey Bobby Coonan was equally convinced that his mount would have won. 'She was jumping perfectly at every fence,' he said. 'She jumped the third-last just as well, but she keeled over on landing. I cannot understand it.' The riders of the main English protagonists – The Dikler and Into View, in third and fourth places – reported that the going had defeated them. 'The ground was bottomless,' according to Barry Brogan, who claimed The Dikler 'hated it'. Said Kelleway*: 'Into View was never going in the rain-sodden ground; he's a racehorse not a hunter.'

Guest was content enough as he led the winner in and prepared once again to receive the cup from the Queen Mother, but the circumstances of the race – combined with two outstanding performances earlier in the week – meant that, even as a dual Gold Cup-winner, L'Escargot secured only a share of the post-festival limelight. The previous day the brilliant Bula had ended Persian War's three-year reign as hurdles champion. On the festival's opening afternoon, meanwhile, L'Escargot's former Colonial Cup rival Crisp had emerged from his first English winter to storm away with the Two-Mile Champion Chase by a remarkable twenty-five lengths against what was by no means the worst field assembled for that test of speed and jumping accuracy. If Dan Moore was to bring his star chaser back in 1972 to attempt the hat-trick, there was a very good chance that Crisp would be on the starting line waiting for him. And of course L'Escargot would be back, fitness permitting. For now, though, journalists preferred to focus on something else Moore had said while basking in the warm glow of his charge's latest victory. 'He jumps like a National horse,' the trainer exclaimed, to owner Guest's evident approval. Next season, then, given a fair wind, there seemed a good chance that L'Escargot would be aimed at the Gold Cup–National double – a feat achieved only once

* Kelleway had won the 1969 Gold Cup riding What A Myth for Captain Ryan Price.

in horseracing history, by Golden Miller in 1934. With such a daunting target in his sights, it was hardly surprising that the master of Ballysax should be attempting to draw a line under other distractions. Moore, reported the *Irish Field*, was 'not keen for L'Escargot to continue his globe-trotting habits, considering that American fences are too soft for him and therefore encourage him to become a sloppy jumper.' This would need Guest to agree to turn his back on his champion's still considerable transatlantic earning potential – and perhaps resist political pressures to dedicate his prize jumping asset once more to the promotion of American steeplechasing – in order to pursue the dream that had tantalised him for nearly fifty years. It was a sign of the strength of Aintree's hold that the trainer got his way.

Of course, it might have been a different story had the 1971 Grand National gone according to plan. Guest must have been cautiously optimistic, with one of his recently acquired Liverpool runners, Cnoc Dubh, in particularly good form. The eight-year-old had appeared on course to win the 3-mile National Hunt Handicap Chase at the Cheltenham festival, only to crash out, like Kinloch Brae and Glencaraig Lady, at that treacherous third-last fence. Frustratingly, in a thrilling National run on fast ground on the first Saturday in April, it was a case of the same old Aintree story for the Guest-owned duo. Neither finished, although Smooth Dealer, with Arthur Moore up, for a time flattered to deceive as one of the leading group. Cnoc Dubh and Carberry parted company at the fence after Valentine's, one fence before the demise of the much-fancied Lord Jim, winner of Cnoc Dubh's race at

Cheltenham. Smooth Dealer lasted until early on the second circuit, coming down at the big open ditch on the run-up towards Becher's. Among other erstwhile rivals of L'Escargot, Twigairy was brought down at the first fence, while King Vulgan did well enough to inspire the thought that he could have challenged on softer ground; he finished eighth. Having packed Leap Frog away for the summer, Jim Dreaper came very close to winning the National for Ireland for the first time in thirteen years. In the end, he and his mount Black Secret were pipped at the post by John Cook, riding holiday-camp entrepreneur Fred Pontin's Specify. Cook threaded his way past four rivals with a very late run.

With America seemingly off the agenda and good going likely, Dan Moore decided his Gold Cup winner had one more race in him before the jump season ended. He would make the short trip to Fairyhouse to run in the Irish Grand National on 12 April. It would entail carrying a punishing top weight of 12st 7lb but enable the trainer to test his thesis about L'Escargot having the attributes of a National horse. With the winner standing to receive almost £10,000, thanks to the largesse of Irish Distillers, the potential financial rewards were appealing too, although Moore was careful to empha-sise that the horse would be considerately ridden. 'He takes his chance, is as well as ever he has been, has quite a stiff task and is a good horse,' he said when confirming that Guest's Gold Cup winner was a definite starter. 'Naturally, if this task proves too much for him in the closing stages, Tommy Carberry cannot be expected to be too hard on such a great and genuine runner.'

L'Escargot was not the only star name to be attracted to the Easter showpiece. After missing out on his own crack at the big Cheltenham prize in unfortunate circumstances, Spanish Steps would join Carberry's mount on the starting line. There were plenty of other plausible contenders among a strong field of nineteen. In this category were Arthur Moore and King's Sprite, who would be receiving the small matter of 36lb from the top weight, 3lb more than in February when they had finished ahead of him in that Leopardstown quagmire. The up-and-coming Dim Wit was another fancy, while Cnoc Dubh provided a second string to the Ballysax bow. The Aintree faller would be ridden by Mick Ennis, who spent much of his working life looking after L'Escargot.

Perhaps mindful of his 12lb weight advantage over the dual Gold Cup winner, punters sent Spanish Steps off as clear favourite at 3/1. Confidence in the English raider may also have been bolstered by the knowledge that he would be ridden by John Cook, the Grand National-winning jockey of just nine days earlier – clearly a man in form. It might, nonetheless, be argued that the market was ignoring the evidence of history: the last English-trained winner of the race had been the fast-finishing Don Sancho all the way back in 1928.*

Blessed with the novelty of bright sunshine on their backs, the field was led off to a steady start by the always-game Proud Tarquin. With L'Escargot held up, Peter McLoughlin's mount was still ahead of a bunched field after one circuit. There had

---

* Don Sancho's jockey was Tommy Cullinan, who rode Billy Barton to second place at Aintree that same year, when Raymond Guest was bitten by the Grand National bug.

been few casualties up to this point, but as the pace quickened, with L'Escargot and King's Sprite moving up from the rear, the drama started. At the fifth-last obstacle – surprise – down came Spanish Steps, taking the unlucky Herring Gull with him. Cook later reported that Edward Courage's horse was 'all out at the time'. The next fence claimed Dim Wit as he was coming to challenge, while the third from home accounted for Cnoc Dubh. By this time King's Sprite and L'Escargot were chasing down the leader, but he plugged doggedly on until a bad mistake two out cost him several lengths. As Arthur Moore recalls, 'I winged the second-last and was gone.' Even then, the gallant Proud Tarquin fought back to within one and a half lengths at the winning-post, with L'Escargot – thwarted by his heavy burden but going down with all guns blazing – just three-quarters of a length further back.

It amounted to a highly satisfactory conclusion to another landmark season. Arthur had emulated his father by riding the winner of an Irish Grand National, the country's richest steeplechase. The handicap had done for L'Escargot, but his reputation had, if anything, been enhanced by the manner of his defeat. It was time now for the luxury of a summer free of flat-racing and transoceanic travel. If all went according to plan, the next season would see him stake his claim to a place among the all-time greats of the sport. But that was a big 'if'.

Chapter 18

Going for the double

On 8 May 1971, as L'Escargot was settling into the least demanding out-of-season routine of his career to date, a Charlie George screamer won the FA Cup – and hence English football's mythical 'double' – for league champions Arsenal. It was only the second time the feat had been accomplished in the twentieth century. All being well, the 1971–72 jump-racing season would see Raymond Guest's gelding attempt to pull off a sporting double of comparable magnitude by becoming only the second horse to win the Cheltenham Gold Cup and the Grand National in the same season.

Sport, though, rarely follows anyone else's script for long – especially in a discipline as anarchic as steeplechasing. A dry start to the autumn, and consequent hard ground, was soon putting trainer Dan Moore's renowned phlegm to the test. Races pencilled in for the gelding's seasonal debut, at Punchestown on 13 October and Newbury ten days later, were ultimately passed up, with Moore saying only that his chaser's future programme would be 'played by ear'. It was not until the end of the month that the master of Ballysax felt able to outline publicly a plan of action for his stable star. L'Escargot would probably run at Fairyhouse on 3 November in the 3-mile Donaghmore Handicap Chase. He could then be considered 'possible' for the Mackeson Gold Cup at Cheltenham and 'probable' for the Hennessy Cognac Gold Cup at Newbury. Moore also confirmed the ambitious late-season target of a third-consecutive Cheltenham Gold Cup followed by a tilt at the Grand National.

The trainer might have preferred a shorter trip than 3 miles for L'Escargot's first outing of a possibly career-defining season. He would almost certainly have appreciated a pound or two less than the 12st 7lb that had been loaded onto the champion's back. Nonetheless, as the leaders approached the final fence, his Wednesday afternoon could not have been going much better. One of the yard's lesser lights had won an earlier maiden hurdle; another had been beaten by only a neck in the novice chase. Now, in front of the small midweek crowd, not only was L'Escargot fighting it out in front with one of his regular adversaries, Proud Tarquin, but another Ballysax horse, the light-framed but lightly weighted Veuve, was coming with a strong run, under the urgings of Moore's son Arthur, in what was his first appearance over 3 miles.

Then, in a couple of seconds, the afternoon – and possibly the entire season – was pitched on its head. L'Escargot, perhaps feeling the lack of a previous race after his unwontedly long summer break, met the fence wrong and came crashing down. Worse – the fall drew blood: Raymond Guest's gelding returned to the unsaddling enclosure with it streaming down a foreleg. The stable won the race, with Veuve staying on impressively to score by five lengths, but just for a few minutes this must have been the least of the Moore team's concerns. Happily the damage turned out to be superficial and Arthur was able to enjoy a finely executed victory aboard a horse he remembers as 'very classy' and 'well named after a lovely wine'.* It was the second-consecutive race of L'Escargot's that Arthur had won. Afterwards, the unhurt Tommy Carberry reflected with wry humour that his mount 'would probably have got over if I had asked him to stand off, but with 12st 7lb on his back I thought I would let him fiddle it – and fiddle it he did.' Typically, Carberry dusted himself off and rode the winner of the next race.

With only ten days' recovery time before the Mackeson, and the weather continuing on the dry side, Moore judged it expedient to sidestep the Cheltenham feature, which was won for Fred Rimell by Terry Biddlecombe on the effervescent Gay Trip. Instead, L'Escargot headed for Newbury for the first time to take his chances in the Hennessy, over the Cheltenham Gold Cup distance of 3¼ miles. The race's timing that year, at the end of November, was perfect. With the days zipping by, and a bit more moisture around, top trainers were finally bringing their big guns out from under wraps. But their absence had made space for new names such as Grey Sombrero and Bighorn to assume prominence in the meantime. The promise of a clash between members of the old guard and this new generation on one of English steeplechasing's pre-eminent

---

* Veuve Clicquot champagne.

tracks had the media licking their lips in anticipation. There was talk of a 'classic'. Some inevitably predicted the 'kind of thrills and excitement more associated with the days of Arkle and Mill House'.

Thirteen runners ended up going to post, with the betting market showing plainly just how open a race was expected. One of the old guard, the 1969 winner Spanish Steps, was sent off as joint favourite at 6/1 with the favourably handicapped Grey Sombrero. Bighorn and Young Ash Leaf were a point longer at 7/1, while L'Escargot – giving more than 1st to most of the talented field and as much as 34lb to the front-running Grey Sombrero – started at 10/1. Even Lucky Edgar, the rank outsider, had his backers at 20/1. Other starters included Proud Tarquin, flying the Dreaper flag, Lord Jim, Royal Toss and the useful Saggart's Choice.

The race did not live up to the hype, which admittedly would have taken some doing. True to form, the dappled Grey Sombrero took them along at a good clip before capsizing four from home. He brought down Royal Toss, while Proud Tarquin was badly hampered, along with one or two others. Spanish Steps had already fallen by this time, breaking jockey John Haine's arm in the process. In an illustration of steeplechasing's severe ups and downs, Haine had only obtained the ride because the horse's regular partner, the Grand National-winning jockey John Cook, had broken a leg in a fall from another horse in Sussex a few days earlier.* Grey Sombrero's demise left Saggart's Choice and Young

---

* This injury would force Cook's retirement.

Ash Leaf at the head of proceedings. David Cartwright, though, had cannily kept the fancied Bighorn out of harm's way towards the rear for much of the race. Before the last, he burst through with an unanswerable run. Though Young Ash Leaf stayed on well, Cartwright's mount was a convincing six lengths clear at the line. 'He went just like a machine,' exclaimed the delighted jockey. The result left one Virginia-based owner to savour the thrill of a victory that was worth more than £6,000 – but it was the American airline pilot who co-owned Bighorn and had flown over especially for the occasion, and not Raymond Guest.

L'Escargot had put in what, even allowing for the handicap, was an uncharacteristically limp performance to trail home sixth, thirty-eight lengths behind the winner. It was quite a comedown for Carberry, who had enjoyed one of the best wins of his career the previous weekend. L'Escargot's jockey had not given up globetrotting even if his dual Gold Cup-winning partner had. He had accordingly flown back out to South Carolina and was able to build on the experience of his previous campaign there to ride Inkslinger, trained by the Moores' relative Mikey Smithwick, to victory in the second running of the Colonial Cup. The inscrutable Moore did not appear too downcast by L'Escargot's failure to mount more of a challenge in Berkshire. Approached in the Newbury unsaddling area, he insisted that he 'wouldn't be a bit disappointed' with the gelding's running. 'He jumped too big and he jumped two or three slow and that kept him out of it,' the trainer concluded. 'But he finished fast, you know he finished all right.'

Commendable realism or rose-tinted spectacles? The answer would become clearer exactly a month later in the suburbs of London, where L'Escargot would contest his first King George VI Chase.* While the pancake-flat Kempton Park course bore little resemblance to Cheltenham, its fences provided every bit as stern a test, and the gelding would be tackling them, as in the Gold Cup, at level weights with most other runners. Held in bright sunshine in front of an enthusiastic and knowledgeable holiday crowd of 19,000 – said to be the biggest in nearly twenty years – it turned out to be one of the races of the season.

Ten runners went to post and at least half were genuine contenders. One of these was that street-fighter Spanish Steps, who had returned to winning ways nine days earlier in a highly competitive SGB Chase at Ascot. The powerful The Dikler was also on an improving path, after finishing a close second to Leap Frog at Cheltenham in a field strong enough to have seen the Irish horse installed as Gold Cup favourite. Leap Frog would not be under orders at Kempton, but the arguably even more talented Irish mare Glencaraig Lady would, alongside L'Escargot. A former winner of the race, Titus Oates, would also be lining up, as would the veteran The Laird and Spanish Steps' stablemate Royal Relief, a top-class 2-miler.

The race got off to quite a start when Even Keel charged to the front, only to crash out at the first fence. Titus Oates took over the lead for the rest of the first circuit, with Spanish

---

* The 1966 renewal had sadly proved to be the great Arkle's last race.

Steps and The Dikler bowling along behind him, followed by the Irish pair. Against his better judgement, Tony 'Geordie' Mawson had Royal Relief tucked in well down the field in the hope that, by conserving energy this way, he might last the 3-mile distance. The jockey would have preferred to let his mount travel at closer to his natural pace and take a chance on him staying on over the final furlongs, but he was following orders. 'If you ride a 2-miler a different way to normal you disappoint him because he wants to go quick,' he explained. Royal Relief, moreover, was capable of winning over more than 2½ miles, as he demonstrated on soft ground at Sandown just over a month later when beating Even Keel and others in the Stone's Ginger Wine Chase. After a circuit ridden at the stipulated slow tempo, Mawson thinks his horse was 'going to sleep'. He goes on: 'He thought it was a school-ing day. He was fiddling fences not pinging them because he wasn't going fast enough.' Coming to the fourteenth obstacle, the jockey remembers that the low late-December sun was shining through a large tree located to the right of the track. 'You couldn't see the fence,' he recalls. 'So I moved onto the outside to get a sight of it. Glencaraig Lady came out of the pack at the same time as I did and ran in front of me to go further outside. It took Royal Relief's eye. He didn't see the fence and walked straight into it.'

Turning for home, the race seemed to be between the trio that had largely set the pace since Even Keel's fall. Jumping the penultimate fence, Titus Oates and Spanish Steps bumped into each other, inflicting a cut on the latter's hind pastern and handing the advantage to Barry Brogan and The Dikler. The impetuous giant, receiving 7lb from most of his rivals, including Spanish Steps, was two lengths to the good as he cleared the last. But the Edward Courage horse was not giving up. As author Michael Tanner painted the picture, 'All the way up that 250yd run-in the burly little bay inched tigerishly closer to his massive Lambourn opponent… with each animal's partisan supporters giving vent to full-throated encouragement.' As they crossed the line, The Dikler retained the edge but only by half a length. It was a result to whet the appetite for Cheltenham. Though still far from foot-perfect with his jumping, L'Escargot had clearly progressed since Newbury, finishing fourth, just half a length down on the tiring Titus Oates and eight lengths behind The Dikler. If they met again at Cheltenham, Dan Moore's horse too would be 7lb better off. Glencaraig Lady came in just behind the Ballysax representative in fifth spot.

In contrast to Kempton, it was a foul day across the Irish Sea at Leopardstown, reducing the huge crowd that would otherwise have turned out to witness a historic moment for Irish racing. Seventy-three-year-old Tom Dreaper was quitting at the top, handing over the reins at Greenogue to Jim, his twenty-year-old son. As was to be expected, he finished in considerable style, registering a four-timer. His most impressive winner was a young chaser called Colebridge, who got the better of Arthur Moore and Veuve. It was a daunting prospect for everyone else in Irish racing: not only was there a new generation of Dreapers on the scene but, in Colebridge, the stable's firepower included the nephew of the great Arkle.

Chapter 19

An instant dislike to Aintree

In the first weeks of 1972 word broke that Raymond Guest was further reining in his Irish interests. Vincent O'Brien would not be training for him in the next flat-racing season. Instead, Guest's European flat operations, it was expected, would mainly be handled from France. While the decision no doubt reflected his changed personal circumstances, it might be argued that the former US ambassador timed his move astutely. The island was entering a dark period: the *Irish Field* printed the story on 29 January 1972; the following day would be etched into history books as Bloody Sunday.

With L'Escargot installed inevitably at the top of the Grand National handicap, Guest also chose this moment to indulge himself by acquiring another likely Aintree type. Ashville was a big, genuine horse with loppy ears who had won two low-key races in quick succession in October. Rather than base him with Dan Moore, Guest left the horse with

Harry Thomson Jones,* known to everyone as Tom Jones, a Newmarket trainer with particularly strong connections in the USA. The Jones-trained Clever Scot had been the only British horse to participate in the 1971 Colonial Cup, finishing ninth in a race won by Tommy Carberry and Inkslinger. Jones himself had bought Ashville on Guest's behalf in Ireland. 'Mr Guest asked me to buy a horse for him with a view to winning the National,' he explained.

Meanwhile, the fickle North Atlantic weather was wreaking havoc once more with racing plans of the main Cheltenham contenders. Whereas in the autumn the problem had been lack of moisture, now, more typically, there was too much of the stuff. L'Escargot had been expected to prepare for his Gold Cup hat-trick bid by running at Fairyhouse on 2 February in the 2½-mile Amberwave† Chase, followed by the Leopardstown Chase later in the month. But at first light in Ratoath on 31 January the racecourse was carpeted with snow. This forced postponement of the meeting by five days. It then emerged that Jim Dreaper had decided to divert Leap Frog to the rescheduled Fairyhouse race from his expected engagement at Sandown Park. Rather than countenance such a clash of the titans more than a month ahead of the main event at Prestbury Park, Moore directed L'Escargot instead

---

* Jones is best known as the trainer of Tingle Creek, a handsome and exuberant 2-mile specialist who also ran in the 1971 Colonial Cup, finishing fifth after leading for much of the race.

† Amberwave won the 1926 Irish Grand National and was third-favourite at Aintree in 1928 when Freddie Guest's horse Koko fell spectacularly at Becher's Brook.

to Leopardstown for the 1972 running of the Foxrock Cup on 5 February. Whereas Leap Frog won very comfortably from Arthur Moore and his regular partner King's Sprite, L'Escargot and Carberry found themselves in what was to all intents and purposes a match-race against an opponent receiving an almighty 41lb.

L'Escargot had already encountered the feisty grey Esban, another son of Escart III, more than a year earlier, just prior to his trek to South Carolina, in the 1970 Irish Cesarewitch. Both had been unplaced. On that occasion, there had been twenty-four runners; this time there were just three – and the other horse, French Alliance, crashed out at the second fence. It was a dismal day with the going extremely heavy. After lead-ing for a mile, Carberry tucked his mount in behind his only rival, but found that the grey was jumping continually out to his right. This made passing him again a lot more difficult in the prevailing conditions than it otherwise might have been, and L'Escargot never managed to do so, crossing the line four lengths in arrears, the bulk of the deficit conceded in the final strides. Though Carberry objected, he was overruled. In truth, the result may have mattered more to Esban's connections than to L'Escargot's. Less than two weeks later, the winner was bought for £10,000 at Ballsbridge by the singer Dorothy Squires.* While Esban went on to run in the Leopardstown Chase, finishing third – albeit not in the singer's red, green and gold colours, which she had not thought to bring to

---

* Squires also came to own Norwegian Flag, the horse that had given Bobby Beasley his comeback victory.

Dublin with her – L'Escargot didn't. After his arduous if unsuccessful 3-mile workout in the early-February mire, Moore had decided it made sense to spare his star another tough pre-Cheltenham battle. According to the trainer, 'the horse is in fine form and does not need another race'. The veteran handler contented himself with sending half a dozen horses, including L'Escargot, to Baldoyle for a workout ahead of his team's departure for Gloucestershire. The now nine-year-old gelding was understood to have come through a fairly strenuous 14-furlong gallop on the flat with flying colours.

The first day of the festival did much to vindicate the sage of Ballysax's judgement. The first three home in the Leopardstown Chase all ran in the Cotswolds. None won, and only Esban came anywhere close to fulfilling reasonable expectations. The biggest flop was the novice Sea Brief, a hugely impressive winner of the Foxrock showpiece less than a month earlier. Sent off as clear 6/4 favourite for the Totalisator Champion Chase, the big youngster laboured home fourth, tasting defeat for the first time in his short steeplechasing career. Jim Dreaper acknowledged afterwards that his charge had probably had too severe a race for a novice in Leopardstown and was 'over the top'. He added: 'I was a bit worried as he walked round the parade ring very calmly – he always pulled his lad round with him. The sticky going was not in his favour either.' The horse's owner, Anne Duchess of Westminster, had a consolation of sorts when she unveiled a bronze statue of Arkle, her greatest champion.

Sea Brief's race was won in fine style by none other than Clever Scot, the Colonial Cup also-ran. Thirty-five minutes later, the Tom Jones team and jockey David Mould* had a festival double after Jomon cruised home in the 3-mile handicap chase. Disappointing here was the Moore-trained Veuve, the Leopardstown Chase runner-up. He could finish no better than seventh in the hands of Carberry after some indifferent jumping. This was three places behind the gritty Esban.

After this surprising first day, it developed into a vintage festival, even if the going remained soft throughout. Pendil announced himself. Bula confirmed his standing as a worthy successor to Persian War. Raymond Guest's new horse Ashville managed to come in second in the Mildmay of Flete. There were glimpses too of two worthy rivals from L'Escargot's past – Kinloch Brae and Garrynagree. They finished respectively second and third in their races. The sun shone, the crowds were large and vociferous and, with new sponsors on board, many of the purses were up. Last but not least, the Cheltenham Gold Cup provided a pulsating finale.

Unlike the previous year, just about everyone you would have wanted to be in the line-up had made it to Prestbury Park. Crisp, Fred Winter's exciting Australian import, was sent off as favourite at 3/1 on the strength of a recent victory over King George VI winner The Dikler at Kempton Park. This was in spite of ground still reckoned to be too yielding for his liking. L'Escargot and Leap Frog were inseparable at 4/1, with Glencaraig Lady, whose experiences at Cheltenham had to this point been less than happy, two points longer at 6/1. The mare's jockey, Frank Berry, would be enjoying his

* Mould was deputising for Stan Mellor, who had caught chickenpox.

first Cheltenham ride. King George VI duellists Spanish Steps and The Dikler were priced at 10/1 and 11/1 respectively, with the battling Royal Toss as long as 22/1. Even the outsiders in the field of twelve were big names with solid reputations: Bighorn, Gay Trip, Titus Oates, Young Ash Leaf and Dim Wit.

After Gay Trip had towed them along for much of the way, at a pace too hot for Dim Wit, most of the action was crammed into the final stages. First, five out, Leap Frog tumbled out of contention in a fall heavy enough to injure jockey Val O'Brien. 'He didn't like the ground,' O'Brien remembers. 'He fell at the last ditch. I don't think he would have won.' Soon afterwards The Dikler, the giant chestnut with the white forehead, made his move under Barry Brogan. Glencaraig Lady and L'Escargot remained in close attendance rounding the bend at the foot of the hill, with the dual champion at this point going as well as anyone. Approaching the penultimate fence, however, Carberry's mount began to veer right, much as he had in the final stages of the 1971 race. As then, he lost most of his momentum, but this time – though his rider got him going up the hill again well enough to reclaim one of the places he lost while clambering over the jump – three rivals, The Dikler, Glencaraig Lady and the fast-finishing Royal Toss, had profited from the champion's mishap and burst clean away. In a thrilling finish, Berry, showing great composure, grabbed the rail and pushed on with the winning-post looming to overhaul the English horse and apparently seize the £15,000 first prize. Royal Toss got up to claim second almost on the line. The drama was by no means over, however. For the first time in the race's history, the stewards had to deal with an objection by one of the main protagonists – Royal Toss's jockey Nigel Wakley. In fact, there were two objections, with third also objecting to second. Twenty nerve-shredding minutes ticked by, and Brogan wrote subsequently that 'speculation in the weighing room was firm that Frank would lose the race'. Eventually, though, the original placings were confirmed.

Everything prior to the stewards' inquiry had happened very quickly. The Ballysax team must have switched in seconds from preparing to roar their star home up the hill to wondering what had gone wrong. A disappointed Carberry summed things up in just two words, saying that L'Escargot 'went cold'. By the time Glencaraig Lady's victory had been confirmed, the astute Moore would probably have ordered his thoughts and concluded that if there were to be more English glory days for his much-decorated campaigner, they were more likely to come at Aintree than Cheltenham.

Exactly three weeks later, L'Escargot embarked on the short hop to Liverpool by plane with four other Ireland-based runners. These included Arthur Moore's mount Miss Hunter, an Aintree veteran. She had finished third in the 1970 Grand National and was, her jockey says, 'strong as an ox'. The lengthening interval since the last Irish winner of the race, in 1958, was really starting to rankle and the 1972 raiding party numbered double figures. Despite carrying top weight of 12st, L'Escargot was seen as the likeliest Irish winner, along with the Dreaper-trained Black Secret, the previous year's runner-up. But the great Aintree showpiece is a unique assignment. Besides needing to have luck on your side, there are what Donald Rumsfeld might have called certain 'known unknowns' that must be answered whenever a horse, however classy, first tackles the race. Will the debutant take to the big, dark Aintree fences? This remains a key imponderable today; it was still more of an issue half a century ago when the fences were bigger and stiffer. Having said that, victory was not completely impossible with a horse that did not feel at home: the great Golden Miller made his distaste for Aintree plain yet won the 1934 renewal in a record time. The other question that hangs over the victory aspirations of Grand National newbies cannot be finessed: will the horse get the gruelling 4½-mile* trip? The Ballysax team could not have known the answers to these questions on 6 April 1972, as the chestnut gelding settled for the first time into his stable in the shadow of the Aintree stands, even if the impressive versatility he had displayed throughout his career to date gave them grounds for optimism.

Carberry and Dan Moore had had quite a week of it already. The Irish Grand National had been run before its English counterpart that year. On heavy ground, Carberry and Veuve had the race snatched away from them when falling at the penultimate fence while leading. The next day, though, brought a bizarre reversal of fortune in the Power Gold Cup – a race Carberry won on a horse called Frou Frou after no fewer than three rivals had come to grief at the exact same fence. Poor Raymond Guest, meanwhile, was having to miss his star steeplechaser's first crack at the Aintree fences. The ex-ambassador was recuperating after an eye operation. In light of what transpired, this might almost be termed a blessing in disguise.

---

* Today's Grand National is slightly shorter than in L'Escargot's day.

The Saturday after Easter was a truly foul day on Merseyside, with the forty-two Grand National runners setting off at just after 3.15pm into driving rain. Since L'Escargot was known to act better on soft ground than most of those perceived as his chief rivals, notably the 1970 winner Gay Trip, this would not altogether have displeased the Ballysax contingent. Punters were certainly wise to the ramifications: while Gay Trip eased from 10/1 out to 12/1, L'Escargot's odds shortened markedly until he was sent off as 17/2 favourite. Money also poured in for champion jockey Graham Thorner's mount, Well To Do, which started at 14/1. Miss Hunter was a 50/1 shot. As was the trend with other races, new sponsorship had sent prize money hurtling upwards. The value to the winner had soared by more than £10,000 from Specify's year and now stood at nearly £26,000.

L'Escargot's race was done and dusted by 3.20pm. At the big open ditch, the third fence, with forty horses charging pell-mell amid the muck and spray down the long straight towards Becher's Brook, he was balked and knocked over by another runner. As he was picking himself up, Gay Trip and Terry Biddlecombe cannoned into his hindquarters. The former winner somehow kept going, and went on to finish second behind Well To Do, but L'Escargot was out of the race. According to Carberry, who escaped from the incident with bruised ribs, his mount 'took an instant dislike to Aintree'. He went on: 'He was very slow over the first two fences and was almost stopping as we came to the third.' Miss Hunter fared somewhat better, covering almost the entire first circuit in second place behind the pony-like Fair Vulgan, before quickly running out of steam after clearing the biggest fence on the course, The Chair. Her rider Arthur Moore recollects, nevertheless, that the mare was 'not really comfortable at all'. She 'wasn't right that year,' he says, adding: 'It was her last year and she was wrong on her back. I pulled her up before Becher's second time around.'

It would have been a dreary way to end the season and, having made it only to the third fence, L'Escargot's handlers were entitled to feel that the gelding had another race in him before the summer break. He and Veuve were both entered for the 3-mile Guinness Chase on the last day of a Punchestown festival blessed with good weather and, hence, firm late-April ground. With Carberry riding his Irish Grand National partner Veuve and Arthur on L'Escargot, both Ballysax horses turned out to be running on empty and were pulled up in a race won by another Aintree starter, Alaska Fort. It was a wretched end to a seriously substandard season for Guest's dual Gold Cup winner.

The latest disappointment ensured that the summer months would be laden with questions of a type that had not previously had to be asked of L'Escargot. After nearly forty tough races – many against opponents of the highest class – had his appetite waned? How might the fire best be rekindled? How would he react if and when he next set eyes on Aintree, where the only really big prize it still made sense to target him at was run?

Guest's other live Grand National hope, Ashville, had been diverted to Ayr in preference to Liverpool after his Cheltenham exertions. Under Stan Mellor, who was nearing the end of a record-breaking career as a jockey, he managed a creditable sixth spot in a good-quality Scottish Grand National field. This was three places back from the hard-working Esban and just one behind a horse called Red Rum.

Chapter 20

Duel

While other members of L'Escargot's entourage were occupied with helping their star recharge his batteries and prolong his remarkable racing career, Tommy Carberry had turned his attentions elsewhere. As the 1972–73 European jump-racing season cranked into action, the Irish jockey was becoming quite the regular transatlantic commuter. August saw him touch down among the elms, petunias and panama hats of fashionable Saratoga Springs. Other 3,000-mile autumn flits took him to Pennsylvania and – again – Camden, South Carolina. His aim? To cement his relationship with Inkslinger, the Mikey Smithwick-trained speedster who had carried him to victory in the 1971 Colonial Cup. For all Carberry's efforts, the five-year-old did not quite match his feats of the previous season on the US circuit. A Marion duPont Scott-owned gelding called Soothsayer rose to prominence, taking both the Temple Gwathmey and the 1972 Colonial Cup, beating Inkslinger by two lengths in the latter. If the jockey's energetic globetrotting did not at first pay quite the dividends he might have wished for, however, his enterprise was rewarded richly once the horse took up residence in Ireland after completion of the US season.

After the first of these Carberry expeditions, L'Escargot was coaxed back onto the racecourse at Listowel, a little riverside town with a fifteenth-century castle in the Irish west, about 40 miles south-west of Limerick. This was to be the first of three appearances in the Kerry National, a much-loved 3-mile chase that was one of the chief focal points of the last of the country's holiday race meetings. While the race had a farcical start, by the time it was over, trainer Dan Moore was left with grounds for cautious optimism. If handled the right way, Raymond Guest's horse might yet attain the new goals that owner and trainer were setting for him.

There were only four other runners in the race, but the handicap as usual was crippling for the dual Gold Cup winner. He conceded 32lb to the best of his opponents, Beggar's Way. Two of the others received 3st exactly, while Culla Hill got a monumental 48lb. They were running on firm ground, which helps to explain why L'Escargot was sent off nonetheless at 5/2 joint favourite of three. No one wanted to set the pace, so much so that the *Irish Field* reported that when the starter pressed the handle, 'for a few moments not one of them moved'. After this pregnant pause, they set off at 'nothing better than a walk.' By the third fence, Carberry had had enough and hit the front, a lead he held until the final stages. The funereal pace may have done little to animate spectators, but it seemed to benefit L'Escargot in one important respect: he was jumping well and showing no propensity to veer right. The finish brought further encouragement: on the run-in, Guest's gelding was travelling by far the best, in spite of the spirit-sapping weight disparity. He failed by just half a length to overhaul the lightweight Culla Hill. Given a few more strides, he would surely have won. A relieved Moore professed himself 'very pleased' with his charge, while no doubt beginning to think through the season that now presented itself. Carberry, for his part, declared the exercise 'as good a school as you'd do'. He upgraded the compliment as soon as it was out of his mouth. 'In fact,' he asserted, 'it was the best preliminary he ever ran.'

The choice of L'Escargot's next race made clear the priority that was to dominate his last two and a half years as a racehorse. This was to end his owner's litany of failures in the event that had tantalised him for so long – the Grand National. Rather than dispatch the chestnut gelding back to Newbury for a tilt at the Hermitage Chase on 21 October, where Spanish Steps would be lying in wait, Moore opted to hold off for another week and seize the chance to go back to Liverpool.

The Ballysax trainer would have realised he was fortunate that this opportunity even existed. As the seemingly endless background rumblings over the Aintree course's future dragged on, there had been no autumn meeting at Liverpool since 1965. In 1972, as the Topham family's long reign over Aintree edged inexorably towards its conclusion, it was decided to have one. The timing just so happened to be perfect for Moore and L'Escargot's purposes.

The horse's miserable Grand National experience the previous April meant that his connections still had no idea if he would take to the unique Aintree fences. If anything, Carberry's post-race report might have encouraged a pessimistic view. By entering him for the William Hill Grand National Trial over a fraction less than 3 miles, with Becher's Brook and all those other mythical obstacles needing to be jumped, they would find out. What is more, though the race would provide a stiff test, there would be less pressure and less general chaos than during the National itself with its forty-plus runners. In the event, a more than useful field of eleven was attracted. These included Specify, the 1971 winner, Black Secret, twice in the frame, and Fair Vulgan, long-time leader of the race L'Escargot had been knocked out of. Gyleburn, quietly fancied when becoming another early casualty in that 1972 National, was also back for a further crack. It had been a second-consecutive dry autumn and, while Guest's horse was top weight, the firm ground ought to ensure that if he jumped well, he would stand every chance.

And so it proved, up to a point. A lightly weighted 16/1 shot called Glenkiln led from start to finish, making it a great day for local trainer Donald 'Ginger' McCain, octogenarian owner Noel Le Mare and jockey Jimmy Bourke,* whose birthday and wedding anniversary it was. But L'Escargot, ridden patiently by Carberry, took the course and all its terrors in his stride to finish an untroubled second. As to a large extent at Listowel, it was one of those days when the nature of the nine-year-old's performance was much more

---

* Bourke would go on to ride Esban to victory in the 1973 Scottish Grand National.

important, at least to connections, than the result. As Moore was to comment some weeks later, 'that race proved that he can jump the Aintree course'.

L'Escargot's handlers would still have to take it on trust on 31 March that he would get the Grand National's ultra-demanding 4½-mile trip. In the meantime, it made sense to keep him as fit as possible. Less than two weeks after his fruit-ful excursion to Aintree, therefore, he was in action again.

The Donaghmore Chase was the race with which he had started his disappointing season the previous year. He had fallen at the last and cut his leg. There was little risk of the 1972 renewal evoking disagreeable memories, however. This was largely because it would be run at a different course – Punchestown instead of Fairyhouse. The Ratoath venue had undergone extensive works, including installation of a new drainage set-up, over the close season. Because of the extended dry spell, the track had not yet recovered to the point where it was deemed ready for racing. Interest in the race was at a high pitch, but this was explained less by L'Escargot than the reappearance of Anne Duchess of Westminster's Sea Brief nearly eight months after his Cheltenham flop. A third horse, the useful Highway View, was dispatched as favourite in a small field of five. Guest's gelding would be giving nearly 2st to the market leader and 20lb to Sea Brief. Trainer Jim Dreaper confided afterwards that he thought the horse in the yellow and black Arkle colours was 'short of work'. He none-theless cruised to a bloodless victory. L'Escargot did loom up fleetingly with a challenge at the last, but Sea Brief jumped it better and, in the words of one report, 'nonchalantly shook off the threat'. Once again, though, the Ballysax chaser had done nothing to discourage his handlers from the belief that he was heading in the desired direction. Ten days later, on the other side of the Atlantic, Carberry had to be content yet again with second place as he and Inkslinger attempted unsuccessfully to defend the Colonial Cup.

The jockey would still have been jet-lagged when Moore let it be known that L'Escargot would be returning to Haydock Park on 29 November to run in the Sundew Chase, named after a former Grand National winner. Sundew triumphed in the Liverpool showpiece in 1957, at the third attempt, ridden by Fred Winter.* It was now more than twenty months since L'Escargot had won a race. But the Lancashire course had brought out the best in him on his only prior visit, in January 1970, when he romped home from East Bound in the inaugural Wills Premier Chase. Having said that, his recent four-length defeat by Sea Brief was put firmly in perspective four days before his Haydock date when the Dreaper horse again disappointed in a big race in England, trailing home sixth in the Hennessy Cognac Gold Cup.

Intense head-to-head duels add savour to sport. There had been a gripping example of this throughout that summer, when chess players Boris Spassky and Bobby Fischer locked horns in Iceland in an extended battle so fierce it took on the aura of the Cold War in microcosm. In European horseracing it rarely happens; there are too many other runners. This was

---

* Sundew subsequently broke his shoulder at Haydock and was buried there.

not the case that Wednesday afternoon beside the M6 motorway. And with L'Escargot up against Spanish Steps – a fellow chaser he would encounter no fewer than ten times over their distinguished and largely contemporaneous careers – this was about as close to Fischer versus Spassky as a six-minute National Hunt steeplechase can get.

There were two other – good – horses in the race: the veteran The Laird and Bighorn, impressive winner of the previous season's Hennessy. Yet for various reasons, not least because L'Escargot would for once not be conceding lumps of weight to his opponents, they were not expected to feature. Indeed, the conditions of the race meant the Irish visitor would be receiving weight from his three adversaries. Given that L'Escargot had placed higher or survived longer than Spanish Steps on four of the five occasions they had met on the racecourse up to this point – the exception being the 1971 King George VI Chase – this did not augur well for the Edward Courage horse's prospects.

Half a century on, jockey Tony 'Geordie' Mawson's memory of the day and of his race aboard Spanish Steps is still so vivid it takes up ten pages of my notebook. He tells me he had actually expected to go into the race with a 5lb weight advantage. So when he found himself instead giving L'Escargot 5lb, it 'took the wind out of my sails'. After some discussion over tactics, it was decided that Spanish Steps would try to make the running. '[Spanish Steps] was the best jumper of a steeplechase fence in the world,' explains Mawson. 'He was just brilliant. If there was a chink in [L'Escargot's] armour, we would find him out and put him on the floor. That was the only way I thought we were going to beat him.' The jockey was also operating under instructions not to hit his horse. He recalls: 'I accepted that because the Gold Cup was his objective. This was probably the first season he had been trained just for the Gold Cup, rather than trying to pick up every handicap on the way.' He remembers Carberry approaching him to ask how he intended to ride. 'I said, "I'm making it, Tommy – and I'm not hanging around."'

Mawson's description of the race, even after so much time, feels almost as if he is riding it again. 'When I came out of the gate, the only thing I had in my mind was, "Get him settled, but watch the first fence because it has a drop on it." You had to turn a bend into the back straight, downhill into the fence. Half a dozen strides before the fence I gave him a pull to get him on his hocks. He pinged it. All the way around he jumped impeccably – a brilliant, brilliant ride. A couple of times Tommy Carberry came up alongside me, but if I got half a length, he dropped back. Then I thought, "I have to get a breather into this horse." I took a little pull and switched him off. Carberry came alongside, then just cruised away from me – like a Formula One car leaving a Mini. He had a gear I thought we had not got. In the straight I changed my hands and suddenly the gear I didn't think we had was there. I said, "Just peg him back over the four plain fences." I went after him very quietly. I passed him just before the last. Mick Batchelor* had told me years before how to ride

---

* Another jockey, who finished second in the 1957 Grand National, riding Wyndburgh.

Haydock. He said to jump the last in the middle. It used to have an elbow in those days. I jumped it in the middle and said, "I will cut Tommy out. I won't let him up the inner." Carberry was a really good jockey. He came around on the other side. Spanish Steps was idling in front. I picked the stick up but didn't hit him because of my instructions. I kept him going, but there was no acceleration. I tried to push Carberry wider and wider, but it wasn't really working. I should have put the stick down and rousted him, driven him with hands and heels… I thought on the line we had won. We pulled up. Tommy turned around right-handed. I counted the weal marks on L'Escargot's backside. He had seven.' He goes on: 'It was a wonderful, wonderful race. A thrilling race to ride in. This power-horse. He was just something else. I hadn't ridden him in a race for four years. I was immensely excited. The thrill of sitting on his back.'

Mawson remembers it took a long time for the outcome of the photo finish to be called. 'They announced it. I could not believe I got beat,' he says. The image showed just how tiny the margin was. 'I always said he beat me by a fat lip,' the jockey continues. 'Normally I would have unclipped that photo and taken it home, but I was so disappointed I left it there.'

Spanish Steps, he says, was a horse whose behaviour was shaped the day after a race by whether he thought he had won or lost. 'When he got beaten, he would be standing there sulking. When he thought he had won, he would be jumping and kicking and squealing.' When Mawson entered the Courage yard in the countryside outside Banbury next morning, his mount was jumping and kicking and squealing. 'He was a leader of the pack,' the jockey concludes. 'He was a wonderful little horse.'

Whether Spanish Steps was aware of the situation or not, the result meant that – by the skin of his teeth – L'Escargot had ended his largely encouraging sequence of second places. Under normal circumstances, Dan Moore's mind might have slipped back for a moment to that other exceptionally tight finish he was involved in at Aintree in 1938. He might even have reflected that the balancing of the celestial scales required one or two more such photo finishes to be adjudged in his favour. However, the trainer's thoughts were in all probability caught up in the more banal business of trying to ascertain what exactly had gone on. While his horse and one of his worthiest rivals had been thrillingly foot-perfect over the forbidding Haydock fences, Moore himself had fallen and had to be whisked to the ambulance room for attention to a badly bruised nose. As a result, he had missed most of the race.

Clerk of the course John Hughes, though, was in no doubt as to what he had just witnessed. It was, he exclaimed, 'the best chase I have ever seen at Haydock Park'.

Chapter 21

Best of the rest

Two weeks after Haydock a new face arrived at Ballysax Manor. With the American steeplechasing season over, and the sport there shrinking back to its roots among the rural elite, Tommy Carberry's favourite western-hemisphere partner Inkslinger had been sent over to see if he could adjust to European jump-racing. After a short spell in quarantine, the 1971 Colonial Cup winner was soon put to work exercising on the windswept practice grounds of The Curragh. In keeping with the theory that the jumping style of US steeplechasers – accustomed to hurtling low over soft, American-type fences – would lend itself to European hurdle races, the new arrival was entered for the valuable Irish Sweeps Hurdle at Leopardstown straight after Christmas.

An outstanding field was attracted, including both the mighty Bula and the up-and-coming Comedy Of Errors, but the front-running Captain Christy outraced them all, storming to victory under a bold ride by Bobby Beasley. It was the most notable win by an Irish-based hurdler for some years and a big feather in the cap of Pat Taaffe, the horse's newbie trainer. Inkslinger's owner Martha Jenney, who used to wear a bracelet spelling out the horse's name in tiny diamonds, had travelled over with a party of friends and watched him run well enough to finish fifth. It was noted that the American runner took some flights of hurdles as though they were fences, and so the decision was swiftly taken that steeplechasing would be his future. It turned out to be an inspired choice.

L'Escargot was sent out hurdling too that festive season, for the first time in two years. On his penultimate day as a nine-year-old, he lined up at Punchestown for the Morgiana Hurdle over 2½ miles. Part of the attraction, as at Haydock, lay in the race conditions: Raymond Guest's horse would be running at level weights with more than half of the thirteen-strong field. With this and his hard-earned recent victory in mind, punters sent the Ballysax representative off as 5/2 favourite. Once again, he ran well and was involved in a desperately close finish with a horse called Lockyersleigh, unplaced in that epic Irish Sweeps Hurdle just three days before. This time L'Escargot lost the decision by a short head. The race was a posthumous triumph for Escart III, sire of the first three past the post.

If Dan Moore had seen fit to enter his veteran chaser for a hurdles race, it was presumably because he wanted to ginger up his speed, and hence still had the Cheltenham Gold Cup in mind, even if the main target for the season was the Grand National at Aintree. So it came as a surprise when, early in the new year, the trainer warned that Prestbury Park might be off the agenda. Guest, Moore said, was 'so keen to have a Grand National winner that we may not send the horse to Cheltenham for fear of injury'. By this time, though, the former ambassador's visits to Ireland were so infrequent that communication with those handling his racing interests was not always straightforward. This was to have significant consequences for the horse in future. Later in January, the message changed. There had been 'consultations' with L'Escargot's owner. In the course of these, the thought had cropped up that since, in the *Irish Times*'s words, the gelding would 'have to have a race into him before Liverpool, Cheltenham may be the best place for him'. Connections held firm to this resolve even though the dual Gold Cup winner subsequently put in his first really disappointing run of the season. This came in a Leopardstown Chase won by Sea Brief for the second-consecutive year, with the hard-grafting Lockyersleigh in second place. Carberry reported that his mount – carrying top weight, but only by one pound over Dim Wit – had made an early mistake and then lost all interest in the race.

Moore, meanwhile, had thrown Inkslinger in very much at the deep end as the American champion set out on his European steeplechasing career. Having no doubt taken soundings from his cousin, Mikey Smithwick, who handled the horse in the USA, the Ballysax trainer had entered him for the Thyestes Chase, one of the sternest examinations of stamina Irish racing has to offer, especially when run on soft ground. Carrying a crushing 12st 7lb and ridden by L'Escargot's day-to-day handler Mick Ennis, Inkslinger finished well down the field at Gowran Park. He nonethe-less pleased his new entourage with his efforts to defy the handicap, admitting defeat only in the last few furlongs. The Ballysax team's mood was further lifted when Arthur Moore cruised to victory in the race, riding Veuve. In what amounted to a crash course in steeplechasing in the British Isles ahead of Cheltenham, the American newcomer was then dispatched with Carberry to Newbury for a very different test, the Newbury Spring Chase over a touch more than 2 miles. There were only two other runners. One of them, Tingle Creek – another US import already starting to win fans in his new surroundings – was familiar to Inkslinger. The other, Pendil, was still unbeaten over fences and considered red-hot favourite for the 1973 Cheltenham Gold Cup. The Fred Winter-trained prodigy duly eased home by seven lengths – but Moore's new charge was proving himself a fast learner.

Just how fast would become clear at Cheltenham. Entered for the Two-Mile Champion Chase on the festival's opening day, Inkslinger found himself up against no fewer than three previous winners of the race – Straight Fort, Crisp and Royal Relief. Crisp was very much the hot tip, at odds of 8/15, yet did not at any stage look like winning. Carberry and Inkslinger took it up from Straight Fort at the penultimate fence, forced the fast-finishing Royal Relief wide on the bend, and held on to win by three-quarters of a length.* That performance in itself was remarkable enough, but two days later Inkslinger and Carberry were back, beating Tingle Creek among others in an underpopulated Cathcart Challenge Cup, the last race

---

* His triumph would have meant the world to Moore, who had trained Quita Que to win the very first running of the race in 1959.

on the card. American steeplechasing might be going through difficult times, but this was plainly nothing to do with the quality of its champions.

About an hour and three-quarters before Inkslinger completed his double, L'Escargot lined up for the Cheltenham Gold Cup for the fourth and final time. With good going and the front-running Charlie Potheen in the field, conditions were in place for an exceptionally fast race. Spanish Steps was there; so was The Dikler. Yet few doubted that the uphill dash to the line would culminate with the coronation of Pendil, the odds-on favourite, as best chaser in Britain and Ireland. Charlie Potheen was, in jockey Terry Biddlecombe's words, 'a wild ride'. Nonetheless, when he jumped the second fence he stood off so far and achieved such height that nearly a decade later this experienced rider wrote that the memory of that moment still 'stirs my blood'. He was still leading when they came back in front of the stands, at which point Clever Scot crumpled, giving Richard Pitman on Pendil a bit of a fright. 'I had to quickly snatch Pendil's head round, hoping his body would follow to avoid the prostrate horse, which luckily it did,' the jockey later remembered, adding: 'Disaster had been only inches away.' Climbing up to the top of the hill, Carberry, who had been riding a patient race, got L'Escargot moving smoothly up the outside into about fourth place. By the time they swooped back down to the final turn, he was poised on the tiring Charlie Potheen's shoulder, perfectly placed. When Pitman made his move and Pendil quickened, however, it was immediately apparent that L'Escargot could not follow suit. A slow jump at the penultimate fence and the three leaders –

Pendil, The Dikler and the labouring Charlie Potheen in front – were away from him. After clearing the last, the favourite looked to have the race in his pocket. Then, as the Cheltenham roar hit him, he seemed to freeze. As Pitman recalled, 'the whole race suddenly became a nightmare'. As Pendil's momentum ebbed, Ron Barry and The Dikler had flown the last and were putting in a storming finish near the inside rail. According to Pitman, Pendil 'rallied to fight for the lead' but 'the winning post came a second too soon'. L'Escargot ran on well enough to claim a share of the prize money in fourth spot ahead of Garoupe and Spanish Steps. Moore and his team were pleased enough, believing that the run should set their horse up well for the coming test at Aintree. For The Dikler's connections, persistence had paid off, with victory in their white-faced giant's fourth Cheltenham Gold Cup. Guest and Moore could only hope the same would apply eventually to their nearly life-long efforts to achieve Grand National glory in Liverpool.

The last minute of the 1973 Grand National, with local hero Red Rum coming from the next county to catch Crisp on the line, is among the most familiar clips of horseracing action in existence. It is not dissimilar to the finish that broke Dan Moore's heart thirty-five years earlier. But the 1938 race was not watched live on television by millions of viewers. And there is something both so mesmerising and so emotionally draining about that 1973 finale that sets it apart. Plus it marks the start of the greatest story that the gods who watch over this unique sporting property have ever come up with.

Behind this shimmering memory of two outstanding horses separated by inches after an attritional battle fought out via the adoption of chalk-and-cheese tactics, much else about this exceptional race has faded into obscurity. Most notably, with Mirabel Topham insisting that this would be the last Grand National staged under her management,* doubts over its future had returned with a vengeance. Owners such as Raymond Guest and Noel Le Mare would have feared that it might be now or never if they were to experience the thrill of winning what some still regarded as the world's greatest sports event. Guest had as strong a hand as he had mustered in sixteen years of trying. Besides L'Escargot, Ashville would be sporting his chocolate-and-pale-blue colours. The Tom Jones-trained eight-year-old had delivered a second-consecutive runner-up spot at the Cheltenham festival – this time in the National Hunt Handicap Chase – and was regarded by some pundits as a better National prospect that year than Guest's other representative in the race, the joint top weight.

Another consequence of the way this spectacular Grand National was reduced to a two-horse race for most of the second circuit is that it was not until I started writing this book that I had really concentrated on what happened to anyone else. While Ashville fell early, tripped up by the first open ditch, this meant I had always missed the remarkable last 1½ miles or so put in by the redoubtable L'Escargot. Moore had underlined his faith in the chestnut gelding ahead of the race, expressing confidence that he would be 'very much concerned in the finish'. In reality, there was no way of

---

* The peerless Aintree historian John Pinfold has pointed out that 1973 was 'the first and only time' Mrs Topham entered the winners' enclosure to present the trophy to the winning connections.

knowing if he would keep going for the full 4½ miles with a hefty 12st on his back, even in the fast conditions prevailing. This might be why Carberry allowed him to hunt around well back in the field for the first half of the race, although the jockey said later that his mount had 'jumped all too deliberately on the first circuit'. Going over Becher's second time around – the twenty-second of thirty fences – he was still back in around fifteenth place, well behind Arthur Moore, who would eventually finish twelfth on the 100/1 shot The Pooka. From that point on, L'Escargot turned on the after-burners, streaking through the field, including his old rival Spanish Steps, like Emerson Fittipaldi lapping back-markers in the British Grand Prix. He did last the distance and, while he had left himself with no chance of winning, assuming the front two did not tip up, he crossed the line only about ten seconds behind them, meaning that he too had broken Golden Miller's 1934 record time for a Grand National.

Once they had got their breath back after a thrilling race, Guest and Moore were left with both good news and bad news to digest. Third place was the best result the American had yet achieved; he had even got his hands at last on some Grand National prize money. He and his trainer had proof positive, moreover, that their horse got the trip, possessed sufficient speed to win the race in a normal year and was young enough to return for a third crack in 1974. Set against this, the new champion, Red Rum, was two years younger than L'Escargot, and – while their 23lb weight differential would be far smaller, perhaps non-existent, in future years – the Irish horse was unlikely to be granted the weight advantage he would perhaps need in order to turn the tables. And that all assumed that there would be a future of any sort for the Grand National.

For now, the positives outweighed the negatives – just about. What is more, the horse had come through this most searching of stamina tests looking so well that for a time it appeared he might run in the Whitbread Gold Cup. This idea was ultimately abandoned in favour of a more straightforward trip to Fairyhouse, where he lined up in a classy-looking field for the Irish Grand National on 23 April alongside stable companion Inkslinger. Here it became plain that his Aintree exertions had taken more out of him than connections had thought. Ridden by Arthur, he was never among the front-runners and finished well down the field. Carrying top weight, Carberry and Inkslinger could manage no better than fourth.

It was an anti-climactic end to a season impossible to condense into a single adjective. Highly encouraging for the way L'Escargot had arrested his decline, it was also not without an undercurrent of frustration. In a way, the Aintree run encapsulated the entire campaign: good, exhilarating even, but not quite good enough. It left plenty to build on – but would Moore and his horse of a lifetime get another chance to prevail in the Liverpool showpiece?

Chapter 22

Something different

'Grand National safe for another five years' was the main takeaway from a press conference at London's Savoy Hotel in November 1973. Mrs Topham had agreed to sell the course for £3million to the Walton Group, a property development company headed by a bearded thirty-eight-year-old called Bill Davies. There were still question-marks hanging over this or that, but Raymond Guest and Dan Moore could breathe a sigh of relief and continue plotting yet another campaign to win the race that had eluded them both for so many years.*

By this point in the season, L'Escargot had already had two unexpected setbacks. The first came in Listowel, where he was again entered in the race that had appeared to reawaken his appetite for jumping the previous year – the Kerry National. As in 1972, there were just five runners; as in 1972, the handicap was punitive, with Guest's gelding attempting to give

---

* There was nothing inevitable about this reasonably happy denouement for horseracing fans: it was less than two months since the *Irish Field* had carried an article headlined 'It seems goodbye to Grand National'.

between 34lb and 42lb to the other four. This time, though, there had been some rain and the ground was considerably softer and – after another slow start – an exciting race developed in front of a bumper County Kerry crowd. Carberry took L'Escargot to the front over the third fence, and much of the 3-mile contest consisted of a duel between him and the Mouse Morris-ridden Rough Silk, with the Ballysax resident again exhibiting his jumping prowess. The pace was not quick enough to shake any of their rivals off, however, and approaching the last fence barely five lengths separated the full quintet, with a mare called Vibrax now at the head of affairs. Her lead proved short-lived: with the race at her mercy, down she came, leaving the 1971 winner Pearl Of Montreal* to gallop on to victory. Vibrax was not the obstacle's only victim. Most uncharacteristically L'Escargot was also tripped up there, with one report saying he 'landed almost on his head'. It was a worrying moment. Carberry later explained that his mount 'took another stride when he shouldn't'. It proved a prelude to an absence from the racecourse for the dual Cheltenham Gold Cup winner that was much longer than initially planned.

It was not an injury that kept L'Escargot away from racing, however,† but that he had succumbed to an attack of jaundice. By the time Bill Davies and Mrs Topham agreed their deal, he

---

* This was a more than useful Kerry National field. Both Pearl Of Montreal and Rough Silk would go on to acquit themselves well in the 1974 Grand National, with Pearl Of Montreal pulled up three from home after running prominently on the first circuit and Rough Silk finishing fifth.

† Although the wording of one brief report suggests that this was suspected. On 23 October, the *Irish Times* told readers: 'L'Escargot, who fell at Listowel, did not sustain a leg injury. He has had one of our human complaints'.

was said to have recovered. 'He looks great,' said Moore just days ahead of the news of the Grand National's latest reprieve. 'We are looking for a suitable race for him.'

The experienced trainer decided to stick to the route that led up to his old campaigner's greatly improved Grand National showing the previous March. In the week between Christmas and New Year, the chestnut gelding made the short trip to Punchestown racecourse for a second appearance in the Morgiana Hurdle. It went about as well as could have been expected. About to turn eleven and running in his fifti-eth race, L'Escargot's waning acceleration was exposed on the run-in in heavy ground, though he held on well enough to take third place. Winner Yenisei, moreover, was a hurdler of some distinction: he had finished fourth just two days earlier in the Irish Sweeps Hurdle at Leopardstown and would go on to be third behind Lanzarote and Comedy Of Errors in that season's Champion Hurdle.

As Moore strove to improve his charge's fitness and make up for the time lost through illness, a third setback struck. The Ballysax veteran was due to return to Leopardstown on 12 January to take on the up-and-coming Spittin Image and Castleruddery when Dublin was hit by its worst storm in seventy-one years. With winds gusting to as much as 112 miles per hour, telephone poles were uprooted and two people lost their lives. The racecourse facilities at Foxrock sustained damage and the meeting was abandoned. A photo-graph published the next morning shows John Gibbons, the course foreman, resignedly assessing the condition of the photo-finish mirror that was blown down in the gale.

It was not until 1 February – by which time Bill Davies and the BBC had reached agreement to televise the Grand National – that Moore was able to get more race miles into L'Escargot's legs. The gelding would make his one and only career appearance at Sandown Park. The venue was in absolutely sparkling condition, its brand new £2.5million grandstand having been opened with due pomp and ceremony by the Queen Mother only the previous September. The country at large was in a sorry state, however, suffering the candle-lit, blanket-swaddled evenings of the three-day week. That year's Gainsborough Chase, over 3 miles, took on the characteristics of a veterans' reunion. In addition to L'Escargot, the field of six included fellow eleven-year-old Into View and twelve-year-olds Titus Oates and Royal Toss, but victory went to the baby of the party, Kilvulgan, aged just seven. The gloss was taken off the win for connections, however, when they saw that he had returned to the paddock seeping blood from a deep wound to one of his hind legs. L'Escargot's fourth place, some six lengths behind a winner to whom he was conceding 5lb, satisfied his trainer well enough. After all, as he pointed out, 'it is some time since our horse raced over fences'.

Three weeks later, Leopardstown's photo-finish mirror was back in its correct position, though the ground was still soft, as the gelding lined up for his fourth Leopardstown Chase. Burdened with a none-too-generous 11st 6lb, he was not really expected to feature, being allowed to set off at odds of 16/1 – much longer than he would carry into any of his four Grand Nationals. Ridden by Arthur Moore, he duly trailed in sixth of eight, just behind Pearl Of Montreal, in a race won in superb style by the Jim Dreaper-trained Lean Forward, a half-brother of the Cheltenham Gold Cup winner Fort Leney. His regular rider, Peter McLoughlin, who also looked after him at the Greenogue yard, remembers Lean Forward as a lovely horse and a brilliant jumper. The race also featured Inkslinger, whose season had somehow not quite taken off to the extent that his magnificent debut year in Europe had suggested might be possible. Under Carberry, he shouldered his 12st top weight honourably enough into third place but showed nothing to indicate that he would be able to match Pendil in the Cheltenham Gold Cup less than a month later. Fred Winter's horse had already beaten him convincingly in the King George VI Chase right after Christmas. This impression turned out to be well founded, with Inkslinger falling relatively early in the championship race. For the second year running, Pendil missed his coronation, this time being brought down by High Ken three fences from home. The mishap left the way clear for Captain Christy to complete one of the great comeback stories in sport for his jockey Bobby Beasley, fifty years after the race's inaugural running.

For the first time in the decade, L'Escargot had not participated in the blue-riband event. But he was there at Cheltenham, and around an hour and a half later he entered the parade ring along with the other runners for the Cathcart Challenge Cup, the festival's final race. Regular racegoers watching the horses circulate – and still buzzing, no doubt, over Beasley's apotheosis and Pendil's bad luck – might have noticed something different about the old Irish champion. For this, his fifty-third race, he was decked out in headgear.

Arthur Moore gives credit for this to Mikey Smithwick, Inkslinger's former trainer in the USA, who was over for Cheltenham. 'He said, "That horse needs blinkers",' Moore recalls. 'He would put the head up. It made sense.'

While Dan Moore had successfully targeted this race before, the Cathcart was very much a case of 'after the Lord Mayor's show': final-day festival attention was riveted invariably on the Gold Cup and perhaps the Daily Express Triumph Hurdle. Beasley's fairy-tale ensured, of course, that this year was no different, yet there was something about the 1974 Cathcart that set it apart and made it a special occasion in its own right. It was to be the last race ridden by Terry Biddlecombe, the former champion and most charismatic jump jockey of his generation. With daylight beginning to fade, the race began and ended with a tumultuous tribute from the remaining spectators to this popular sportsman. Biddlecombe admitted that as he passed the winning-post for the last time, 'tears blinded my eyes' and tiredness 'swept over me'.

There was a pronounced American flavour to proceedings. Biddlecombe's final ride had been on Amarind, runner-up in the 1971 Temple Gwathmey.* A big chestnut, he was now based with Fulke Walwyn in Lambourn. He had attempted the same double that was achieved by Moore's Inkslinger the previous year, only to capsize in the Two-Mile Champion Chase on the festival's opening day in what Biddlecombe described as a 'thorough bone-shaker' for horse and rider.

---

* Smooth Dealer, one of Guest's entries for the 1971 Grand National, also ran in this race.

Not surprisingly, he could manage no better than fifth two days later in the Cathcart. Another veteran of the US steeplechasing circuit fared rather better: Inkslinger's old Colonial Cup rival Soothsayer had also come over to Lambourn, to be trained by Fred Winter. Sent off as a warm 11/8 favourite, he duly obliged, handing punters a farewell present for the journey home and owner Marion duPont Scott a Cheltenham festival winner thirty-six years after Battleship's great Aintree triumph.

As in 1938, Moore had to be content with second best but, unlike then, he would have been happy to do so. In spite of the sharp 2-mile trip, L'Escargot delivered his most convincing performance since his illness, crossing the line four lengths behind Soothsayer, with another former festival-winner, the two-years-younger Clever Scot, six lengths further back in third place. Whether his new headgear was responsible or not, Guest's chestnut gelding looked to be coming back to the boil just in time for his next trip to Liverpool two weeks later. There seemed much grounds for optimism. After all, impressive as Red Rum's 1973 victory had been, you had to go back even before Battleship – to Reynoldstown in 1935 and 1936* – to find the last horse to win two consecutive Aintree Grand Nationals.

---

* In the 1936 Grand National, Reynoldstown was ridden by none other than Fulke Walwyn.

Chapter 23

The one to beat

One interested spectator at the 1974 running of the Cathcart Challenge Cup was Brian Fletcher. Red Rum's jockey took good note of the strong run by the horse carrying the chocolate-and-pale-blue colours, as became clear a couple of weeks later when he was asked to nominate the main threat to his mount at Aintree. 'Last year that horse was a mile behind and he got up to finish third,' Fletcher told the *Liverpool Echo*'s Charles Lambert. 'I saw him at Cheltenham the other week over 2 miles when he was equipped with blinkers for the first time, and they really sharpened him up. That's the one to beat.'

A certain amount of razzmatazz accompanied this first Grand National meeting under Bill Davies's stewardship. Aintree's new owner had the good idea of reviving Jump Sunday, a tradition – abandoned in 1960 – of allowing people to walk the course, typically on the weekend ahead of the meeting, to marvel at the outsized fences and imbibe the history of the place. To enhance the appeal, a fairground was set up, as well as what one newspaper described as a 'Petticoat Lane-style market'. Members of the Nottingham Jousting Association were even on hand, giving demonstrations of a different kind of horse-sport, while a planned parachute display by the Red Devils had to be called off because of low cloud. The developer's plans for expanding the sports offering on the site were at this point extremely bullish. There was talk of five horseracing meetings instead of one in 1975 and of the return of international motor-sports.* Davies even bought a horse, rejoicing in the name of Wolverhampton, that took part in the 1974 race. Sporting the businessman's black-and-white colours, the seven-year-old was reasonably well backed at 25/1 but was pulled up.

L'Escargot alone would be flying Raymond Guest's flag in the Grand National this time around. The American, though, also had an interest in the Topham Trophy, run over one circuit of the giant, spruce-dressed Grand National fences on the first day of the three-day meeting. This was the race to which Ashville, a third-fence faller in the 1973 National, had been assigned. Sadly, the Aintree obstacles again proved too much for him, and he came down at the biggest fence on the course, the fearsome 5ft 2in open ditch called The Chair. The Dan Moore-trained mare Frou Frou fared rather better, finishing fifth and giving jockey Tommy Carberry an early spin over the fences he would again be tackling with L'Escargot that coming Saturday.

---

* Aintree staged the British Grand Prix five times between 1955 and 1962.

With Liverpool bathed in sunshine on 30 March, the morning of the race, it was clear that Red Rum – the local horse trained on harrowed sands near the Royal Birkdale golf course – would get the fast ground his handlers craved. He would be shouldering 23lb more than when he had won 364 days earlier, while L'Escargot would carry 1lb less. This, together with the thought that Guest's horse may have had more in the tank when finishing third in his last attempt, gave grounds for reasoning that the twenty-five-length margin separating them on that occasion might be surmountable. Then again, the Ginger McCain-trained horse, still only nine, had been in splendid form all season, winning half of his eight races, and losing the Hennessy Cognac Gold Cup by the shortest of short heads. Of the other runners among the forty-two-strong field, the Fred Rimell-trained Rough House and Gordon Richards-trained Straight Vulgan were rated solid prospects, while the ever-willing Spanish Steps could never be counted out. Also in the line-up were San-Feliu, once a victor over L'Escargot in a yuletide hurdle race at Leopardstown, and another Escart III foal, the Dorothy Squires-owned Norwegian Flag, with his one prominent white sock. Though never in the picture, both were to perform creditably enough, finishing ninth and tenth respectively.

If the sunshine accentuated the finery of the jockeys' silks as they made their way out of the weighing room towards their mounts circulating in the parade ring, it also showed up the prominent advertising hoardings around the perimeter to good effect. Davies had, moreover, cannily stationed what was billed as the world's largest advertising poster site on the sparsely populated embankment overlooking the course on the way down to Becher's Brook. There is no doubt that the sense of a new era dawning – with, as the *Irish Field* put it, the 'fur coat image of veteran owner Mrs Mirabel Topham replaced by the fat cigar of property tycoon Bill Davies' – helped to perk up interest in the race. One bookmaker predicted that between £8million and £10million* would be wagered on it. But recession was taking its toll on the British economy at large, and a tax-raising budget – including a hike in betting tax from 6 to 7.5 per cent – unveiled that week by the new Labour Government would further hit discretionary spending. With massive capital investment required on the Aintree venue's infrastructure, it was not going to be easy for Davies, or anyone else, to secure the course's long-term future – irrespective of what new development plans might be unveiled. At the same time, it beggars belief in our age of scrupulously staggered major sports fixtures that this 1974 Grand National should have clashed directly with an FA Cup semi-final featuring one of the big local football teams, Liverpool. As Red Rum, L'Escargot and the others paraded ahead of the off, that match, being played 30 miles away in Manchester, had just got under way. With more sensible scheduling, it is hard not to think the crowd on the embankment beneath Davies's world-beating poster site might well have been more numerous.

As the minutes ticked down ahead of the cavalry charge to the first fence, Carberry and L'Escargot looked almost

---

* Equivalent to well over £100million today.

preternaturally calm. While most of their rivals fidgeted, these veterans of over forty races together in three different countries waited impassively by the rail. The still-unfamiliar blinkers, held in place by a band of indigo cloth stretched across the gelding's forehead above the wholly familiar sheepskin noseband, did not seem to bother him. He can see 'less of the local scenery than usual', remarked master-commentator Peter O'Sullevan dryly for the benefit of TV viewers. Shortly before the start, a rivulet of punters' cash staked on Guest's placid horse sent his odds tumbling to 7/1. For a minute or two he was outright favourite. Then, as sometimes happens, an even later and more pronounced gamble on a particular runner – in this case the lightly weighted Scout – transformed the market. From 12/1, the price on Tommy Stack's mount nosedived to sevens, while L'Escargot edged out again to 17/2. 'They're under starter's orders and Tommy Stack will not know that he's riding the National favourite,' O'Sullevan observed, as another runner, Princess Camilla, indulged in an uncooperative jig.

Away they went, and it was quickly apparent that Carberry's tactics were altogether different from the previous year, when he had been scarcely visible for the first circuit. This time, confident that his mount would get the marathon trip, he was up among the first half-dozen almost from the start – and well before Red Rum put in an appearance. The experienced jockey was riding to win, which also meant saving every yard he could. For most of the race, therefore, he steered a technically demanding course hugging the inside rail. Absolutely nothing was inside him the first time over the

Canal Turn, where a sweetly angled leap can redeem several lengths. This was just as well, as the obstacle claimed several victims. L'Escargot fiddled the fence and found himself slightly squeezed. But the partnership was still intact and very much in the vanguard.

At The Chair – the fifteenth fence and hence the halfway point in terms of jumping efforts – L'Escargot was second or third. He was tucked in behind Pearl Of Montreal and level with an outsider called Charles Dickens, owned by a well-known amateur jockey Lieutenant-Colonel Sir Piers Bengough, but being ridden by the stylish professional Andy Turnell. Approaching Becher's Brook on the second circuit – the twenty-second fence – Charles Dickens and L'Escargot were still second and third, but Pearl Of Montreal had dropped back. Red Rum had cruised through the gears and the field, and had now taken it up, sooner than Fletcher would ideally have wanted. The favourite, Scout, had also made up good ground in the local horse's tracks. With Red Rum, L'Escargot and Spanish Steps all among the top five at Valentine's Brook, the twenty-fifth fence, it seemed clear that while a new era might have dawned in some ways, the old guard was still very much in the driving seat when it came to the race itself. Red Rum was down on his nose at the next fence but recovered scarcely without breaking stride. Soon after this, Scout ran out of steam, leaving it to the other four – the big three and Charles Dickens – to fight out the closing stages. Over the long run to the penultimate fence, Red Rum and L'Escargot broke away, with Spanish Steps unable to quicken and Charles Dickens seemingly at the end of his tether, having run well above expectations. Approaching the obstacle, the gap between the first two shrank to about three lengths. This was as close as Carberry was to get. With just one to jump, Fletcher began pulling away again. The final distance at the winning-post was a comfortable seven lengths. Over the agonisingly long run-in, a different problem loomed for Carberry: Charles Dickens had found a second wind and was closing on his mount at an alarming rate. The two tired horses flashed over the line together. This resulted in a photo finish being called.

In the fuddle of emotions, did Dan Moore's mind flash back yet again to 1938? Did he wish for the thousandth time that photo-finish technology had been available on that day to adjudicate precisely between his mount Royal Danieli and the fast-closing Battleship? I somehow doubt it, not immediately anyway. At any rate, this was quite a big moment for the venerable race – the very first photo finish in its long history. It felt somehow right when the result came and Moore's horse was given the verdict. But how the trainer must have wished that it was to determine first and not second place.

Charles Dickens's entourage had other things on their mind. As Bengough later told author Chris Pitt, the horse's saddle had slipped jumping The Chair, where he was hampered by a loose horse. The owner went on: 'By the end of the race, his girths were back round his stomach. To a certain extent it stopped him breathing. The consequence of that was it strained his heart.' Bengough explained how connections rushed out to the finishing area to find the horse 'very distressed'. They managed to keep the bay walking for about an hour as he recovered, and then gave him a year's rest. The following season he ran in a couple of races in which, according to his owner, he 'went for 2 miles and stopped'. After that, Bengough decided to keep him for hunting.

It was Brian Fletcher's third win in the race, a feat matched by only one other jockey in the twentieth century,* yet he at once told David Coleman, the BBC's star anchorman, that 'anyone can ride a horse like that'. Owner Noel Le Mare cheerfully reminded everyone that next year Red Rum would 'still be in his prime'. Having again beaten Golden Miller's 1934 time, albeit this time by just a tenth of a second, the local horse had now run the two fastest winning times in Grand National history.

As for eleven-year-old L'Escargot, given a fair wind, he could realistically hope for one more shot, but if that did not work out, Guest would probably be obliged to find yet another steeplechaser to go in quest of his holy grail.†

While it was frustrating to be so close to a lifelong ambition without attaining it, the American soon had fresh grounds for optimism as to what his horse might yet be capable of, even with one more year on the clock. L'Escargot's two previous seasons had petered out tamely. However well he appeared after his latest Liverpool sortie, his Ballysax handlers must have feared another anti-climax when he lined up at Fairyhouse

---

* On his retirement in 1976, Fletcher's Grand National record stood at a remarkable three wins, one second and two thirds.

† Three twelve-year-olds – Kilmore, Team Spirit and Highland Wedding – had won the race in the 1960s alone, but the last thirteen-year-old was Sergeant Murphy in 1923.

in mid-April for the Irish Distillers Grand National. It was a race he had come third in three years earlier – and third place appeared the very most that could be hoped for in 1974, with Cheltenham Gold Cup winner Captain Christy and the Arkle relative Colebridge in the field. Even so, the old fellow was not being asked to carry such mountainous weights nowadays, at least not against rivals of high calibre. Having witnessed his so-near-yet-so-far Aintree heroics, punters were prepared to allow that if he ran well with the sun on his back, he had a sniff of a chance. He was sent off at a rather stingy 4/1. Bookmakers would have been congratulating themselves on their prescience when, about a third of the way through the 3½-mile contest, the unpredictable Captain Christy fell.* At this point, a horse called Southern Quest was in the lead. On the run to the penultimate obstacle, the favourite Colebridge assumed command and galloped home under no real pressure for a classy victory. L'Escargot on this occasion rolled up his metaphorical sleeves and finished strongly too. He even rallied again in the last few yards to hold off an effort to snatch second place by the plucky Highway View.

This third-consecutive runner-up spot at flagship meetings capped an excellent late-season revival by the Ballysax veteran. All his handlers could do now was hope that he summered well, retained this restored appetite for the chase and was granted a modicum of luck in what would be his ninth season as a racehorse.

---

* He came out the next day and won the Power Gold Cup in irresistible style with some stupendous jumping.

Chapter 24

A single-minded campaign

Raymond Guest's far-flung horseracing and bloodstock interests provided him with plenty to be getting on with while waiting for the clock to tick around to Grand National time once again. On 4 May – less than three weeks after L'Escargot's 1973–74 season had drawn to a close at Fairyhouse – Guest's chocolate-and-pale-blue colours were doing duty at one of American racing's most historic occasions: the hundredth running of the Kentucky Derby. His colt, Sir Tristram, was among a record-breaking twenty-three-strong field whose owners had paid sharply increased fees to have a runner in the Churchill Downs starting stalls for this highly prestigious race. Queen Elizabeth II's sister, Princess Margaret, was among more than 163,000 spectators who saw Cannonade charge to victory in the Louisville sunshine. Sir Tristram, trained in France but not quite the racehorse that his sire Sir Ivor had been, came in eleventh.*

---

* Sir Tristram went on to be a successful sire in New Zealand.

Six weeks later, Guest was in Paris as one of his Virginia-bred horses, Cutlass, was winning the feature race of the day 3,000 miles away at Belmont Park. As it happened, this was a month when trainer Dan Moore's attention was also on the French capital, with Inkslinger due to line up in the Grand Steeple-Chase de Paris at Auteuil racecourse. Things did not go to plan. As Moore subsequently explained, 'He was going well with Tommy Carberry up until getting a serious shin-bone fracture, and he had to be pulled up. I have left him in a clinic in Normandy, where the veterinary surgeon said after an operation that the gelding should be able to race again after a few months. But the present view of the owner, Mrs Michael Sanger, is that she would prefer to take him home to America for her own use.' This is indeed what happened.

If L'Escargot's 1973–74 campaign had been oriented principally on the Grand National, his racing schedule for the following season was geared entirely to the great Liverpool showpiece. After a long lay-off, he returned to action at his local track Punchestown on 24 October. The 2½-mile Free Handicap Chase looked a big ask, with both the Jim Dreaper-trained Lough Inagh and Captain Christy lining up, even if the 1974 Cheltenham Gold Cup winner was being asked to give L'Escargot 22lb. Lough Inagh sailed home with little problem in what was described disappointingly as a 'somewhat tame affair'. Captain Christy finished fifth, the zip drained out of him in yielding ground by his punishing weight. L'Escargot brushed aside the cobwebs, kept plugging away and recorded the only dead heat of his career, with Argent, for third place. While Guest's chestnut gelding still had one stiff, possibly career-defining, test ahead of him, a new generation was coming to the fore at Ballysax Manor. The Free Handicap Hurdle, run the previous day, had been won by a horse called Tied Cottage.*

Two weeks later, L'Escargot travelled down to County Tipperary to run at Thurles for the one and only time in his career. In the interim, the so-called 'Rumble in the Jungle' – in which Muhammad Ali upset the seemingly invincible George Foreman, seven years his junior, in a heavyweight boxing match at a stadium in Zaire – showed thrillingly what veteran athletes were capable of. This was to be one of those races in which L'Escargot simply refused to take much interest, however. Back under a big weight, he coasted in sixth. At this point in the season, details of the Grand National runner-up's race record were still not terribly high on Guest's list of equine priorities, provided he remained fit and well. Five days after that glorified autumnal training run, the former ambassador splashed $220,000 on a mare in foal to a stallion he referred to as 'the immortal Secretariat'.†

It was, though, a dreary winter for the Irish horse business. The shockwaves from the first oil crisis had left few industries untouched, and this quirky branch of the agricultural sector had not escaped the malaise. A year-ending editorial published by the *Irish Field* under the headline

---

* A newcomer called Monksfield was another winner that day. Not to say that the result was unexpected, but the *Irish Field* noted that the winner 'paid fractionally under 647 to one on the Totalisator to the under half dozen racegoers who invested on him'.

† Secretariat, or 'Big Red', was the peerless winner of the previous year's Triple Crown.

'A Year to Forget' summarised 1974 as 'a year that saw the collapse of the bloodstock market coupled with an unprecedented rise in costs'. Showing a contrarian's instincts, Arthur Moore chose this moment to branch out and set up his own training operation in rented premises in County Kildare, while continuing to race-ride.

It was not until well into February that L'Escargot was seen again on a racecourse. For the third-consecutive year, Dan Moore picked the 3-mile Leopardstown Chase as an ideally timed primer for the big tests at the end of the season. With Carberry suspended, Mick Ennis – the Ballysax 'sonny boy' who knew the now twelve-year-old gelding as well as anyone – took the ride. With the ground heavy and most eyes on the impetuous and top-weight-carrying Captain Christy for clues as to his state of mind and well-being for Cheltenham, L'Escargot cruised around perfectly smoothly without ever promising to get on terms with the leaders. Little Highway View came through to win an exciting contest under Mouse Morris from the 1974 winner Lean Forward. The Captain Christy-watchers were on the whole satisfied with his strong-jumping fourth place. Moore would have been pleased too: a searching examination of his Grand National horse's strength, fitness and appetite for jumping had been negotiated without mishap. Those 3 miles in deep ground would stand Guest's veteran chaser in good stead for the Liverpool marathon just six weeks away. Before then, though, the horse would line up at his eighth and final Cheltenham festival. Like the previous year, when his punchy performance in the Cathcart Challenge Cup had caught Brian Fletcher's eye, the intended focus would be on sharpening his turn of foot.

In the event, the weather was so bad that he might well have had no Cheltenham outing at all. Despite strenuous efforts – with Major-General Sir Randle Feilden, the racecourse chairman, saying that 'all forms of manpower and machinery' were being used to clear surface water – the first day of the three-day meeting had to be abandoned. The race Moore had earmarked for L'Escargot, the Two-Mile Champion Chase, was added to the original day-two programme, and so Carberry and the dual Gold Cup winner were able to go to post some twenty-four hours later than planned, albeit in desperately wet conditions. Very much an outsider in a field of minimum-distance stars such as Tingle Creek and Royal Relief, L'Escargot splashed around safely in fifth place. Just as in his first race of the season at Punchestown, victory went to Lough Inagh.* With Cheltenham so saturated, it was little surprise that the Irish had a successful festival – no one more so than Tommy Carberry. On a truncated final day he drove the Jim Dreaper-trained Ten Up powerfully up the sodden Cheltenham hill to claim his third Cheltenham Gold Cup win and owner Anne Duchess of Westminster's fourth. Marion duPont Scott's Soothsayer got up for a gritty second place with blood streaming from one knee. Former hurdles champion Bula was third. Captain Christy floundered in the extreme conditions and was pulled up.

---

* It was his jockey Sean Barker's very first win in England.

As the rain that had swept in all day over the shoulder of Cleeve Hill turned to snow, Carberry – who had also guided Brown Lad to victory in the previous day's Lloyds Bank Hurdle – sat amid the muddied debris of the weighing room, champagne in one hand, cigar in the other. At the absolute peak of his profession, this brilliant, intuitive horseman well deserved a moment or two of boisterous relaxation in one of steeplechasing's most revered shrines. Had he paused to reflect on life's trajectory since that day nearly two decades earlier when he had plucked up the courage to ask Dan Moore for a chance, he might easily have concluded that this was as sweet as it was likely to get. How wrong he would have been.

Chapter 25

Avoiding the abyss, fulfilling the dream

Champagne had been on offer too at a Central London press conference a month or so before Tommy Carberry's impromptu Cheltenham celebration. Aintree's new owner Bill Davies invited reporters to his company's offices just off Park Lane and favoured them with a flurry of announcements. While some related to the Grand National meeting scheduled for the first week in April, much the biggest stir was caused by Davies's disclosure that he was seeking approval for the Liverpool venue to stage a new £100,000 flat race. This was to be run late in the season, in October. Lord Derby was said to have given his consent for the new event to be called the Aintree Derby. Reaction to the headline-grabbing proposal was mixed – which is more than could be said for the response to another decision unveiled that day: the cost of coming to watch the Grand National was to rise sharply. The *Daily Mirror*'s Tim Richards carefully itemised the new prices.

'Entrance to Tattersalls on Grand National day has been doubled to £12. Other prices on National days are: County Stand £20 (from £15), Silver Ring £8 (from £3.50),' and so on. Davies said: 'We raised prices last year and the National attendance leapt from 36,000 to 40,000. It's the greatest race in the world and we still maintain that even more people will pay the additional charges in April.'*

The 1975 Grand National would certainly have a compelling storyline. The locally trained Red Rum would be trying for an unprecedented hat-trick of victories. In any catalogue of 'I was there' moments from British sport in the 1970s, a third Red Rum Grand National win would rank close to the top. Looking back on events from our vantage point in the early 2020s, what is perplexing – even allowing for the price hikes, even allowing for the deep-seated woes afflicting the national economy and even allowing for another clash with the FA Cup semi-finals – is that tickets to watch the race did not more or less sell themselves.

Having made the frame in both Red Rum's winning years to date, L'Escargot was viewed as one of the chief dangers to fulfilment of the fairy-tale. This contributed to the especially keen sense of anticipation that accompanied publication on 12 February of the weights allocated to horses entered for the race. Raymond Guest's twelve-year-old was allotted just

---

* The *Liverpool Echo* reported that, by contrast, car-parking charges were being reduced to £2 on Grand National day. Jump Sunday would stretch over four days, since it happened to coincide with Easter, with adults charged £1.50 and children 50 pence. £1 vouchers, redeemable against Grand National day admission charges, were to be distributed.

11st 3lb. With Red Rum inevitably at the top of the handicap again with 12st, this meant the Ballysax representative would be 10lb better off than when last challenging the king of Aintree the previous March. These two would not, of course, have the race to themselves. Other much-discussed imposts included the gallant Crisp, the 1973 runner-up, with 12st*; The Dikler – like L'Escargot, a Cheltenham Gold Cup winner – with 11st 3lb; and Spanish Steps, Edward Courage's indomitable warrior, with just 10st 3lb – an advantage big enough perhaps to compensate for the lack of a gear-change apparent in previous efforts.

Red Rum's trainer Ginger McCain was relaxed about the weight assigned to his charge. He had already demon-strated, after all, that he could win with the 12st maximum on his back. What concerned him far more, as a dreary and rain-swept winter dragged interminably on, was the possi-ble state of the Aintree ground. Red Rum had been granted the good going he relished for his two victories to date. This time it was starting to look like he would not be so lucky. Guest and Dan Moore had no such worries: with an 11lb weight advantage over the one horse to have had L'Escargot's measure the previous year, soft ground would suit them just fine. It might suit some of the lightweights in the handicap too, but there were good reasons for their favourable treat-ment. Over 4½ miles and thirty ultra-demanding Aintree fences, there was a strong chance those with the biggest weight advantage would succumb to flawed jumping tech-nique or a deficiency of stamina.

---

* Crisp did not in the end take part in the 1975 renewal.

With a month to go, though, just when the sole focus of the racing industry's attention in Britain and Ireland would normally be Cheltenham, all speculation about the specifics of the race was abruptly silenced.

So many Grand Nationals in the 1960s and 1970s had been run under a shadow of deep uncertainty over the race's future that people had become first accustomed to, then cynical about, the seemingly perennial existential question-mark. That did not lessen the sense of relief when Mrs Topham beat her retreat, leaving the racecourse in the hands of an ambitious new owner. So it would have come as a shock to many in the first week of March 1975 to find themselves again reading the sort of headlines that had become common currency in the bad old days. 'Hopes fading for National,' read one. Some readers must have thought, 'Oh no, not again.' The new outburst of negativity had been triggered by an apparent impasse in negotiations between Bill Davies and the Jockey Club over money, investment and the owner's proposed new Aintree Derby. Suddenly Guest and Moore's latest attempt to overcome their respective Aintree jinxes looked like it might be confounded at the eleventh hour. Assuming he heard the news in France or Virginia, well away from the British racing rumour-mill, Guest's exasperation in particular can well be imagined. Happily, on this occasion, the storm – at least insofar as its possible effect on the 1975 Grand National was concerned – subsided in record-quick time. Within days, the *Daily Mirror*'s Frank Corless was reporting that Davies had backed down. 'I'll compromise... for the sake of the British people,' the businessman pledged melodramatically. The

April race meeting would go ahead 'come hell or high water'. While the first day of the Cheltenham festival was abandoned as a wash-out, Davies was photographed at Becher's Brook with Grand National preparations said to be fully under way.

Carberry's golden run did not end at Cheltenham. On 31 March, the thirty-three-year-old won his first Irish Grand National on Brown Lad. It was a perfect prelude to the race's English counterpart at the end of the same week. First, though, L'Escargot's jockey had another day of racing at Fairyhouse to navigate. Here, in an obscure novice chase with twenty-one runners, disaster almost struck. Carberry's mount, the third-favourite Guiscard, was one of ten fallers.* Carberry sustained a suspected cracked collarbone. He duly sat out the rest of the meeting. It was thought for a time that the injury could jeopardise his presence at Aintree. It was a textbook illustration of the metaphorical tightrope that jump jockeys walk every day of their thrill-a-minute but highly precarious careers. Fortunately, one of Carberry's many attributes was toughness. When the Topham Trophy rolled around two days after his fall, there he was in his assigned place aboard Our Greenwood, reacquainting himself with those big, dark Liverpool fences. Nor was he in any way just making up the numbers: he duly won the race to keep his recent spate of marquee victories going.

While Carberry was flirting with catastrophe, Red Rum's connections were starting to feel the pressure unleashed by

---

* Arthur Moore's mount Inishowen fell too. The race was won by Drumroan, destined to finish third in the 1978 Grand National.

their bid for a remarkable piece of horseracing history. Jockey Brian Fletcher fretted that 'between us... we have used up all our luck in the race'. He went on: 'His chance is obvious, but I can't really see it happening again. To be honest, the pressure has been building up so much in the past few days I wish it was all over.' Nor was the relentlessly miserable weather helping. On a visit to Southport, journalist Jonathan Powell reported snow falling as Red Rum exercised just a week before the race. There was worse to come for both trainer Ginger McCain and Aintree owner Bill Davies as the countdown to the Grand National entered its final hours: on the eve of the big race, Davies's horse, Wolverhampton – a 50/1 outsider also trained by McCain – collapsed and died on the beach after a 4-furlong training spin. A more crushingly depressing omen would be hard to imagine.

On the train to Liverpool for what he hoped would be the last time after a near half-century obsession with the National, Guest was nervous too. He was accompanied by his wife Caroline Murat, who seemed content to double up as a good-luck charm, remarking: 'I think Raymond thinks I might bring him luck because when I went to Epsom twice he won the Derby.' Guest himself acknowledged experiencing what he called 'a sort of a nightmare', elaborating: 'In my dreams I used to think that he might get over the last fence first, but that some lightweight would run by him in the home stretch.' It is tempting to think that this pesky 'lightweight' might have been carrying the famous yellow-and-maroon colours of Edward Courage. His toughest horse, Spanish Steps, would be in that category this year and his rider Bill

Smith was 'totally and utterly convinced' he was going to win. Admittedly, while this may in part have reflected the favourable handicap, his conviction was further underpinned by a good old-fashioned dose of jump-jockey superstition. As Smith explained to author Chris Pitt, he had won a big race that season, the Schweppes Hurdle, on a horse carrying the same number – thirteen – that Spanish Steps would be wearing at Aintree. Furthermore, another ex-Courage jockey, John Cook, had won the National and the Schweppes Hurdle in the same season.

And so the stage was set for a race that Aintree's owner had said would be seen in 155 countries. Whether or not the television audience ultimately matched Davies's expectations, the size of the racecourse crowd was far from worthy of an occasion that might easily have produced one of British sport's most historic outcomes. Somewhere in the region of 12,000 people – about what you might expect for a second-division football match – are thought to have been present to witness Red Rum's first bid for immortality.* Much the best atmosphere looked to be in the vicinity of Becher's Brook. Irish broadcaster Michael O'Hehir, who was stationed there, said the crowds around Becher's were 'the biggest for years'. He contrasted this with the 'handful of dedicated fans reaching into their pockets for the inflation type admission fees'. In an era of powerful trade unions and often tempestuous industrial relations, the crowd would have been a little bigger

---

* This estimate is given following reference to contemporary reports and consultation with Aintree historian John Pinfold.

but for the cancellation of two Liverpool-bound trains owing to an overtime ban by workshop supervisors.

Carberry, who was carrying a small snail's shell entrusted to him by Virginia Guest as a good-luck charm, would not have given two hoots about the size of the audience – not at this stage of the afternoon anyway. He knew he was aboard a horse that could get the job done, and that the handicap and the dead ground were in his favour. He would have noticed too the money pouring in for him and his twelve-year-old mount in the final days and hours before the off. Red Rum, naturally, was prohibitive favourite, at 7/2, but L'Escargot was sent off only three points longer at 13/2. This was the shortest starting price of his four Grand National attempts. In essence, the market was predicting a two-horse race – just like the previous year. Dan Moore had been unwell during the build-up to the race but had made it to Aintree, buoyed by the knowledge of what a good chance he had finally to assuage the disappointment of 1938. A man of few words at the best of times, it is improbable that he would have given his jockey – whom he knew to be in the form of his life and a veteran of ten Grand Nationals already – much in the way of race instructions.

In the crowded parade ring, L'Escargot – familiar by now with everything a day at the races could throw at him – looked a deal more relaxed than his sixty-seven-year-old owner. As Guest periodically whipped off his bowler-hat to greet acquaintances with patrician *politesse*, the chestnut gelding circulated patiently. The most eye-catching aspect of his appearance was a set of blinkers held in place by a mainly light-blue hood. Royal-blue ribbon covered the seams, form-ing a cross on the old steeplechaser's forehead. Nearly fifty years on, it is striking how many people with some recollec-tion of L'Escargot recall this distinctive headgear. It is as if he has passed into posterity wearing them, along with the sheep-skin noseband that he sported in seemingly all his races.

More patience was required of those about to set off on the National's exacting 4½-mile journey when a horse called Junior Partner needed running repairs on a plate. This delayed the scheduled 3.15pm start by a quarter of an hour. When at last the relatively small thirty-one-strong field was placed under starter's orders, another runner, Feel Free – sporting colours deceptively similar to the yellow and black always carried by Arkle – was somehow facing the wrong way. His rider, Marshalla 'Taffy' Salaman, spun him around. A moment later, they were off.

Carberry got L'Escargot out of the blocks every bit as fast as the previous year, and they cleared the first fence in fourth place. The jockey seemed less concerned this time with hewing to the inner. As the field sped past the sparsely populated embankment with its king-sized advertising hoarding, he stuck to a line closer to the centre of the course than the inside rail. If he had hoped that they were in a forward enough posi-tion to secure an incident-free passage while settling into their racing rhythm, he was quickly disappointed. At the second obstacle the reshod Junior Partner took a tumble directly to his left. That did not require Guest's horse to break stride. Two fences later, however, when the early leader Zimulator crumpled and the fancied, Fred Rimell-trained Rough House also fell, L'Escargot had to step inside the hazard. He executed the manoeuvre adroitly enough, but one wonders whether all this Aintree-style aggravation in his immediate vicinity somehow broke his concentration. He jumped Becher's carefully and well to the centre, his old Gold Cup rival The Dikler leaping past him before they touched down. Then, at one of the smallest fences on the course – the site of mayhem eight years earlier, in Foinavon's National – came the blunder that so nearly put L'Escargot and Carberry out of the race.

Terry Biddlecombe was always wary of the fence he called the 'baby hurdle'. Its relatively small size meant, he felt, that it was not respected by the horses. This made it a 'trick fence' or, more colloquially, 'a bastard'. While nothing compares with 1967, a sizeable roll-call of Grand National runners have come to grief there over the decades. These very nearly included Dan Moore's nemesis, Marion duPont Scott's National-winning Battleship – although in his defence it should be underlined that the fence was much bigger prior to changes made in 1955. The obstacle also almost caught out L'Escargot even though the veteran chaser had previously cleared Biddlecombe's 'baby hurdle' five times without problem.

When Battleship met the fence wrong in 1938, it had only been a very sportsmanlike helping hand from fellow jockey Fred Rimell that had kept the little stallion's partnership with Bruce Hobbs intact. When L'Escargot hit it hard, pitched forward and all but catapulted Carberry to an ignominious exit, the Irishman could count on no such assistance. In addition to survival instincts honed through something like a quarter of a century in the saddle, what saved him – and the

Grand National dreams of the men for whom he was riding – was his foresight, and to a degree humility, in adopting an elementary precaution. Carberry had bridged his reins. That is to say he had put one rein over the top of the other to form a loop of leather, in effect a sort of handle, over the top of the horse's neck. The technique can be deployed as an aid to control should a rider want to discourage his mount from pulling too strongly too soon. In this case, as he teetered as precariously as the robbers' bullion-laden bus at the end of *The Italian Job*, it enabled Carberry to avoid falling into the abyss reserved for those whose Grand National hopes have been dashed for another year. Studying the much-reproduced action photograph that was taken, with the jockey's left calf parallel to the ground and his hands not far short of the horse's long ears, the recovery still looks little short of miraculous. O'Hehir called it 'the recovery of his career'.

Carberry claimed later that the error woke L'Escargot up. That is not necessarily the way it looks over the rest of the first circuit. The near-disaster caused a loss of momentum that had relegated him to seventh going over the Canal Turn. From there, Carberry tacked across to the inside rail for the first time, and that was where he stayed along the run of fences heading back towards the Melling Road. At Valentine's Brook – the ninth fence – Glanford Brigg, a horse good enough to have finished fourth in that year's drenched Cheltenham Gold Cup, had the lead, but the yellow diamond on Brian Fletcher's chest was beginning to assume more prominence in about twelfth place. Approaching The Chair – fence number fifteen and the biggest on the course – a cluster of loose horses that had been gradually coalescing at the head of the field swayed this way then that, posing a problem for Glanford Brigg's jockey Martin Blackshaw. Though they cleared the wall-like obstacle without too much discomfort, the curtain of unpredictable horseflesh forced Blackshaw and his mount right over to the stand-side. This created an inviting opening for other members of the leading group – including L'Escargot – to stream into, although Glanford Brigg worked hard to cut back across the course and retain his lead at the water-jump, the sixteenth fence.

Turning to head out for the second circuit, you still would not have said that L'Escargot, lying seventh, was going noticeably more easily than his rivals. The horse directly behind him now was the doughty Spanish Steps, and behind Edward Courage's inveterate battler, Brian Fletcher's bright-yellow cap aboard Red Rum was looming ominously. But this was where Carberry switched back to the centre of the course prior to asking for another gear – and finding it. By the eighteenth, they were in fourth place, with Red Rum also increasing his pace and Southern Quest hitting the front under Sammy Shields. Spanish Steps, by contrast, was finding things tougher than jockey Bill Smith had hoped. 'Going out second time, when you start to get into the race, I wasn't finding it quite as easy as I thought it should be,' the rider later recalled. At the big open ditch, the nineteenth, a stupendous leap by High Ken took him and Barry Brogan into the lead, while Red Rum cruised up onto L'Escargot's shoulder. The local hero continued to make progress and as the leaders approached the fence before Becher's – number twenty-one – four horses were almost stride for stride: the rallying Glanford Brigg on the inner, High Ken, Southern Quest and Red Rum. Carberry, running fractionally ahead of The Dikler, had allowed a two-length gap to open up. This may have been a race-winning decision: it meant that when High Ken came crashing down, L'Escargot had just enough room to sidestep the tumbling blue-and-white-shirted jockey. Brogan sustained a badly bruised left arm in the fall.

For all that this latest close escape displayed the old horse's well-honed survival instincts and enduring agility, it again cost him momentum; when he and Carberry launched themselves warily over Becher's for the second time, in fifth place, they appeared to be losing ground. As was about to become clear, though, the experienced and in-form jockey had the situation under control.

Just after the twenty-third, at the very far end of the course, Red Rum still had Southern Quest in front of him. Yet Fletcher, whose respect for L'Escargot was no secret, took a careful look over his left shoulder in the general direction of Carberry half a dozen lengths behind. If this reflected some sort of intimation that the Irishman was about to make his move, the suspicion was well founded.

Three strides away from the Canal Turn, the seventh fence from home, Carberry wrestles his mount's head to the left. You can see the effort, but his timing is spot on: the old chaser meets the fence on a good stride and a line well to the inside of the quartet preceding him, making up ground without impairing his rhythm. As Red Rum jumps into a narrow lead for the first time at Valentine's, L'Escargot is back on the inside rail, has overhauled The Dikler and is on the tiring Glanford Brigg's tail. After the twenty-sixth, Red Rum still has Southern Quest on his shoulder, yet Fletcher again glances back, only to see his most-feared rival up into third and powering on ever more strongly with that loping, ground-devouring stride. By the fourth fence from home, Raymond Guest's horse has already erased the remaining deficit. The first three touch down together. The race suddenly looks in the bag – except there are three big fences and a mile or more to run.

Over the third-last, and the big two are in the clear. Now it is Carberry's turn to take a long look back, checking for any other possible danger. It might appear to be a titanic duel between two great champions, but it isn't really. Carberry knows by this point that, aided by his weight advantage, he could accelerate away on the dead ground whenever he chooses. Instead, he sits tight beside his toiling rival, takes another long, lingering look back and awaits his moment. Watching them side by side, his long-legged mount looks so much bigger than Red Rum that you might think they should be in separate weight categories. Back in the underpopulated stands, the Guests and the Moores must have known that only a fencing blunder could rob them now. The surviving lightweights were too far back to be a factor. Guest's recurrent nightmare was not going to come true.

A typically economical L'Escargot clearance of the last, and the moment Carberry had been waiting for had arrived. Off they sped towards the Elbow on that long Aintree run-in, putting five, eight, ten lengths between themselves and the best Grand National horse in history. As they crossed the line, with Carberry already beginning to pull him up, the margin was an emphatic fifteen lengths. It can be disorienting when something so hard-won is achieved so comfortably. As Dan Moore – who must have relived and then exorcised half a lifetime's frustration in the final minute of the race – remarked: 'It has taken me thirty-seven years to prove that this place isn't unlucky for me, but it has been worth it.' A weight had been lifted.

Chapter 26

One last grandstand finish

Someone else recognised exactly how special a landmark for Dan Moore L'Escargot's victory had been. A telegram had been received. At a cocktail party in the Adelphi Hotel that evening, Virginia Guest stood on a chair and read it out to those assembled. It was short and to the point, as telegrams generally were unless the sender was made of money. The last sentence read: 'Sorry you didn't ride a National winner – but I'm delighted that you trained one – Bruce.' It was both fitting and generous that the jockey who had pipped Moore to the post on Battleship all those years earlier, Bruce Hobbs, should have had the wit to encapsulate what the day meant for his old rival in just fifteen words. Today such sentiments would get swamped in the Twittersphere.

A gratified Raymond Guest had finally bagged his Grand National – at the thirteenth attempt, no less.* It was perhaps a shame that a Liverpool crowd of 1928 dimensions was not on

---

* He had one attempt by Virginius, two by Flying Wild, two by Packed Home, one by Great Lark, one by Cnoc Dubh, one by Smooth Dealer, one by Ashville and four by L'Escargot.

hand to witness the accomplishment of his mission nearly half a century after the race had beguiled him. It was a shame too that circumstance had cast him and his resolute chestnut horse as party poopers for having thwarted Red Rum's bid for an unprecedented Grand National hat-trick. But, like Arthur Ashe winning Wimbledon a few months later just five days short of his thirty-second birthday, this was an exemplary sporting tale of persistence rewarded. And there would be further opportunities for the gallant runner-up; as his owner Noel Le Mare said after the race, 'We'll bring back Red Rum again next year.'

It was also a first Grand National victory for jockey Tommy Carberry. As he sipped more champagne from a paper cup while talking the press through details of his eventful race with patience and lucidity, he must have wondered if the month-long purple patch that had brought him the Cheltenham Gold Cup, Topham Trophy and both English and Irish Nationals would ever end. As one wit put it, 'There appears little left for Carberry to win aside from the Boat Race and the FA Cup.' One leading bookmaking firm had forecast that a L'Escargot win at Aintree would cost them as much as £100,000. Raymond Guest, it seems, did not have a bet on this occasion and so was not directly responsible for any of those losses. Nonetheless, the £38,000 Grand National prize took L'Escargot's career earnings for his owner to around £88,000 in Britain and Ireland.*

* It is hard to be too precise in translating this to present-day values: L'Escargot's winnings were earned over quite a long period of time for a racehorse and inflation was significant for part of this period. However, very approximately, £88,000 at the time when L'Escargot was active would have equivalent purchasing power of somewhere around £1million today.

A supremely versatile racehorse, he earned more than another $26,000 from his expeditions to the USA.

Remarkably, given the fine record of Irish trainers in the race since the turn of the millennium, L'Escargot was the first Irish-trained winner of the National for seventeen years.* What was even more remarkable was that he had emerged from the very same cut-stone stable complex in out-of-the-way Westmeath as the 1958 winner, Mr What. Having achieved a lifetime's ambition by breeding one Grand National winner, Betty O'Neill sadly did not live to see lightning strike a second time. At least her widower, Arthur, remained to appreciate her extraordinary achievement.

It was the last of fourteen racecourse victories for L'Escargot. His future had been mapped out, after some deliberation, even before he lined up for his final outing over the best-known steeplechase fences on the planet. The plan had been to gift him to Virginia Guest, who would ride him out hunting. At dinner on the eve of the race with Tommy and Pamela Carberry, however, when the topic came up, Tommy remarked that Raymond Guest's daughter might need Muhammad Ali in the saddle with her if she was to be able to hold him. Virginia says: 'I also knew in my heart of hearts that Ballysax Manor was his only home for ten years. I suggested giving him to Joan Moore. It was the right thing to do. I was thrilled. I wanted the horse to be happy.' As Michael O'Hehir recounted, moments

---

* The interval before the next Irish-trained winner turned out to be even longer: twenty-four years. Finally, in 1999, a horse called Bobbyjo again won the race for Ireland. The trainer? Tommy Carberry. The jockey? Tommy's son Paul.

before the race Guest informed his trainer's wife of the decision with the words, 'Win or lose, he is yours from now on to hunt and to give a good time in his retirement.' It must be said that this presented her with an enviable choice of conveyance when she rode to hounds: she had similarly been gifted Team Spirit, the 1964 Grand National winner.

By the time Hobbs's telegram was read out, a weary L'Escargot was already being prepared for a night-flight back to The Curragh, accompanied by Mick Ennis, his occasional jockey and most constant attendant. The next day, they would be up, bright-eyed and bushy-tailed, at Ballysax Manor for the obligatory hero's homecoming/Grand National winner's press call for the Monday-morning newspapers. And that might have been the end of the story, with the chestnut gelding living out his days as a minor celebrity in the Kildare countryside. However, there was to be one final twist.

Racehorses are not machines that can be switched on and off at will. When their racing days are over, the transition to a radically different routine ideally requires attentive management. Even then, it is not always accomplished easily. After a few months of his new regime, the Moores had the clear impression that L'Escargot was missing his racing. When September rolled around, therefore, they decided to enter him for the Kerry National, a race he had run in twice before. As Dan Moore explained afterwards: 'We gave him the run just to cheer him up, without any question of bringing him back into regular training.'

Unexpected though his reappearance may have been, the racegoers of Listowel gave the veteran chaser a hero's welcome

– even if, for his sixty-first and, as it turned out, final race he was carrying unfamiliar green-and-white colours belonging to Joan Moore. He did not let them down. Given a relatively free rein by Carberry, he led from the start until the third-last, giving every indication of relishing his return, until joined by Southern Quest, his old Aintree adversary. He then dropped back, apparently spent, only for Carberry to conjure one last grandstand finish out of him on the run-in. In spite of carrying top weight, he surged back into contention and pushed the winner – a horse called Black Mac – every inch of the way to go down in a photograph. It is stirring to think of him exiting racing in this way, with the roar of a wildly appreciative Kerry crowd ringing in those loppy chestnut ears.

At first, it was reported that the prospects of him running again were bright. Joan Moore was quoted saying, 'That's why we ran him: that's the way he was at home, longing to get back in action.' Then word began to filter through that Raymond Guest was displeased. In October, Dan Moore announced that L'Escargot was unlikely to race again. He acknowledged that he had been 'unable to get in touch with Mr Guest to explain the position to him' but would now do so. The upshot was that this exemplar of Irish steeplechasing was shipped off to take his retirement in Virginia not Kildare.

Looking back, it seems clear that this bathetic coda to the career of one of the great Irish racehorses came about because of a genuine misunderstanding of a sort commonplace in a field of endeavour where decisions can be taken quickly, the course of events is unpredictable and agreements tended not to be written down in triplicate and witnessed by lawyers.

It is true that the widespread presumption in the wake of that cathartic April afternoon at Aintree was that L'Escargot would not race again. Joan Moore is quoted in the *Irish Times* as saying he would never do so. But some contemporary accounts are more nuanced. One talks in terms of L'Escargot's racecourse career being over 'unless some suitably soft race happens to present itself'. Another quotes Raymond Guest saying: 'He won't race again unless Dan decides for some outing for him in Ireland if he gets lonely for the race-track crowds.' In such circumstances, it does not surprise me that the Moores evidently felt they had leeway to send him racing again if they judged it in the horse's interest, as plainly they did. Equally, from Guest's perspective, this was the animal that had enabled him to realise almost a boyhood dream and to experience the thrill of a lifetime. As a man of honour, he would certainly have felt that he owed it to the horse to live out his days in comfort. Whenever he raced, he risked injury or worse; two horses died in that 1975 Grand National. While horses can also injure themselves when out hunting, I can imagine that Guest would have come down hard on himself if the best steeplechaser he had owned sustained a catastrophic injury while racing in old age. Given that there was now an ocean between them, the far-from-seamless international communications networks of the era were a further factor in what happened. You could not just pick up your mobile phone and text your interlocutor in Tierra del Fuego or Vladivostok. Dan Moore is even recorded fretting about communicating with owners in the film about Guest's strivings to win the National, *The Snail, The Diplomat and*

The Chase. 'When trying to let Mr Guest know how the horse is,' Moore says, 'I'm always waiting for another day because when I write to him and post that letter I know that within three days I'm going to do something with him that just might prove wrong... There is that sort of time delay in training and I hate ever putting in a letter, "You'll win, don't worry".'

What most matters, of course, is that the old warrior lived through his declining years in Virginia while being every bit as well looked after as he would have been at Ballysax Manor. 'In extreme luxury with straw up to his hocks in an enormous box stall,' is how Virginia Guest Valentine phrases it.

I like to think of him there, picking at grass and settling slowly back into his adolescent routine of eating and sleeping. Every once in a while, perhaps, memories of a very different life would flood back and, to adapt the poet Philip Larkin's phrase, plague those expressive ears of his like flies. Nearly a decade meandered by before the enormous box stall became available for another resident. Guest Valentine's funny old boy – a winner on both sides of the Irish Sea and the Atlantic, and among the least aptly named horses in racing history – died aged twenty-one, in 1984. He was no snail.

L'Escargot's racing record

61 starts: **1st** 14 **2nd** 15 **3rd** 7

Date	Racecourse	Racename	Length	Type	Jockey	Runners	Placing
1967							
15 February	Navan	Grattan Cup	2mi	flat	Hanbury	22	**Won**
25 March	Phoenix Park	Ashbourne Stakes	2mi	flat	Hanbury	16	2nd
27 April	Punchestown	Cooltrim Plate	2mi	flat	Hanbury	13	2nd
6 September	Tralee	Carling Black Label Stakes	1mi 5f	flat	McEntee	14	Unpl
14 October	Naas	Rathangan Stakes	2mi 1f	flat	Hanbury	17	**Won**
21 October	The Curragh	Irish Cesarewitch	2mi	flat	Boothman	22	Unpl
1968							
2 March	Naas	Osberstown Hurdle	2mi 1f	hdl	Carberry	13	**Won**
19 March	Cheltenham	Gloucestershire Hurdle	2mi 1f	hdl	Carberry	11	**Won**
30 April	Punchestown	Champion Novice Hurdle	2mi	hdl	Carberry	12	4th
22 May	Down Royal	Carling Black Label Novice Hurdle	2mi	hdl	Carberry	9	2nd
28 December	Leopardstown	Tower Handicap Hurdle	2mi 3f	hdl	Carberry	8	Unpl

Date	Racecourse	Racename	Length	Type	Jockey	Runners	Placing
1969							
11 January	Leopardstown	Ticknock Handicap Hurdle	2mi	hdl	Carberry	8	3rd
22 February	Leopardstown	Scalp Hurdle	2mi	hdl	Carberry	10	**Won**
19 March	Cheltenham	Champion Hurdle	2mi 1f	hdl	Carberry	17	Unpl
7 April	Fairyhouse	Power Gold Cup	2¼mi	chase	Coonan	8	2nd
1 May	Punchestown	Colliers Chase	2mi	chase	Carberry	5	**Won**
12 May	Leopardstown	Woodbine Chase	2¼mi	chase	Carberry	5	**Won**
3 June	Belmont Park	Meadow Brook Chase	2½mi	chase	Carberry	12	**Won**
17 October	Belmont Park	Temple Gwathmey	3mi	chase	Carberry	12	3rd
15 November	Punchestown	Sandymount Chase	2½mi	chase	Carberry	11	2nd
26 December	Fairyhouse	Paddock Chase	2¼mi	chase	Carberry	6	**Won**
1970							
17 January	Haydock Park	Wills Premier Chase	2½mi	chase	Carberry	17	**Won**
21 February	Navan	Leopardstown Chase	3mi	chase	Carberry	9	2nd
19 March	Cheltenham	Cheltenham Gold Cup	3¼mi	chase	Carberry	12	**Won**
17 October	The Curragh	Irish Cesarewitch	2mi	flat	Johnson	24	Unpl
31 October	The Curragh	Crotanstown Stakes	1½mi	flat	Carberry	23	Unpl
14 November	Camden	Colonial Cup	2mi 6½f	chase	Carberry	22	4th

Date	Racecourse	Racename	Length	Type	Jockey	Runners	Placing
1970 (cont.)							
28 December	Fairyhouse	Irish Sweeps Hurdle	2mi	hdl	Carberry	11	4th
1971							
9 January	Punchestown	Rathside Chase	3mi	chase	Carberry	6	UR
20 February	Leopardstown	Leopardstown Chase	3mi	chase	Carberry	10	3rd
18 March	Cheltenham	Cheltenham Gold Cup	3¼mi	chase	Carberry	8	**Won**
12 April	Fairyhouse	Irish Grand National	3¼mi	chase	Carberry	19	3rd
3 November	Fairyhouse	Donaghmore H'cap Chase	3mi	chase	Carberry	5	Fell
27 November	Newbury	Hennessy Cognac Gold Cup	3¼mi	chase	Carberry	13	Unpl
27 December	Kempton Park	King George VI Chase	3mi	chase	Carberry	10	4th
1972							
5 February	Leopardstown	Foxrock Cup	3mi	chase	Carberry	3	2nd
16 March	Cheltenham	Cheltenham Gold Cup	3¼mi	chase	Carberry	12	4th
8 April	Aintree	Grand National	4mi 856yds	chase	Carberry	42	BD
27 April	Punchestown	Guinness H'cap Chase	3mi 132yds	chase	Moore	11	PU
26 September	Listowel	Kerry National	3mi	chase	Carberry	5	2nd
28 October	Aintree	Grand National Trial	2mi 7½f	chase	Carberry	11	2nd
8 November	Punchestown	Donaghmore H'cap Chase	3mi	chase	Carberry	5	2nd

Date	Racecourse	Racename	Length	Type	Jockey	Runners	Placing
29 November	Haydock Park	Sundew Chase	3mi	chase	Carberry	4	**Won**
30 December	Punchestown	Morgiana Hurdle	2½mi	hdl	Carberry	13	2nd
1973							
17 February	Leopardstown	Leopardstown Chase	3mi	chase	Carberry	11	Unpl
15 March	Cheltenham	Cheltenham Gold Cup	3¼mi	chase	Carberry	8	4th
31 March	Aintree	Grand National	4mi 856yds	chase	Carberry	38	3rd
23 April	Fairyhouse	Irish Grand National	3¼mi	chase	Moore	14	Unpl
25 September	Listowel	Kerry National	3mi	chase	Carberry	5	Fell
29 December	Punchestown	Morgiana Hurdle	2½mi	hdl	Carberry	6	3rd
1974							
1 February	Sandown Park	Gainsborough Chase	3mi 118yds	chase	Carberry	6	4th
23 February	Leopardstown	Leopardstown Chase	3mi	chase	Moore	8	Unpl
14 March	Cheltenham	Cathcart Challenge Cup	2mi	chase	Carberry	7	2nd
30 March	Aintree	Grand National	4mi 856yds	chase	Carberry	42	2nd
15 April	Fairyhouse	Irish Grand National	3½mi	chase	Carberry	10	2nd
24 October	Punchestown	Free H'cap Chase	2½mi	chase	Carberry	7	3rd
7 November	Thurles	Molony Cup	3mi	chase	Carberry	8	Unpl

Date	Racecourse	Racename	Length	Type	Jockey	Runners	Placing
1975							
22 February	Leopardstown	Leopardstown Chase	3mi	chase	Carberry	9	Unpl
12 March	Cheltenham	Two-Mile Champion Chase	2mi	chase	Carberry	8	Unpl
5 April	Aintree	Grand National	4mi 856yds	chase	Carberry	31	**Won**
23 September	Listowel	Kerry National	3mi	chase	Carberry	11	2nd

Note on sources

With searchable online archives now commonplace, I felt it unnecessary to freight a book such as this with chapter and verse on each and every newspaper reference. I spent much time using three archives in particular: the British Newspaper Archive, and those available to subscribers of *The New York Times* and *Irish Times* respectively. A few of my interlocutors kept scrapbooks covering the period when L'Escargot was active to which I was kindly granted access. When alluding to articles or other items encountered in one of these, I have endeavoured to specify the source, where this was made clear in the scrapbook. One important publication not available online (as far as I could tell) while I was engaged on research was the *Irish Field*. For this I was grateful to the London Library's extensive collection.

I also referred repeatedly to two documentary films. The first, entirely devoted to L'Escargot and those most closely associated with him, was *The Snail, The Diplomat and The Chase*. I am indebted to Revel Guest for granting me access to this. L'Escargot also features in a series about Irish National Hunt horses entitled *Laochra na Rásaíochta*. I was able to access this via the Irish public-service television network TG4's website at www.tg4.ie. Once again, I am grateful to those who alerted me to this.

Dozens of people in at least four countries consented to be questioned or interviewed by me either face to face or via one of numerous media. Several gave up a lot of time to help me along. I am thankful to each of them. For general information, Wikipedia was often helpful. I have made a donation in acknowledgement.

Bibliography

Second Start by Bobby Beasley (London: W.H. Allen, 1976)

Winner's Disclosure: An autobiography by Terry Biddlecombe with Pat Lucas (London: Stanley Paul & Co. Limited, 1982)

The Barry Brogan Story: In his own words by Barry Brogan (London: Arthur Barker Limited, 1981)

Aintree: Grand Nationals – Past and Present by Paul Brown (New York: The Derrydale Press, 1930)

Tales from the Weighing Room: A life in racing by John Buckingham (and John Dorman) (London: Pelham Books Limited, 1987)

One Hell of a Ride: The autobiography by Paul Carberry with Des Gibson (Dublin: Paperweight Publications, 2011)

The Secret War Against Hitler by William Casey (New York: Simon & Schuster, 1989)

Mouse Morris: His extraordinary racing life by Declan Colley (Cork: The Collins Press, 2008)

A–Z of the Grand National: The official guide to the world's most famous steeplechase by John Cottrell and Marcus Armytage (Newbury: Highdown, 2008)

Jump Jockeys 1950–2000 compiled by Chas Hammond (Chas Hammond, 2015)

Arkle: The classic story of a champion by Ivor Herbert (London: Aurum Press, 2003)

'Irish Racing's Peaceable Kingdoms' by Michael Hinds, in *The Cambridge Companion to Horseracing* edited by Rebecca Cassidy (Cambridge: Cambridge University Press, 2013)

The Grand National: The Irish at Aintree by Anne Holland (Dublin: The O'Brien Press, 2008)

The Grand National: Anybody's Race by Peter King (London: Quartet Books Limited, 1983)

Cheltenham Racecourse by Alan Lee (London: Pelham Books, 1985)

Racing and the Irish: A celebration by Sean Magee (London: Stanley Paul & Co, 1992)

My Colourful Life: From Red to Amber by Ginger McCain (London: Headline, 2005)

Britain and Ireland's Top 100 Racehorses of All Time by Robin Oakley (London: Corinthian Books, 2013)

Vincent O'Brien: The official biography by Jacqueline O'Brien and Ivor Herbert (London: Bantam Press, 2005)

Battleship: A daring heiress, a teenage jockey and America's horse by Dorothy Ours (New York: St Martin's Griffin, 2014)

Foinavon: The story of the Grand National's biggest upset by David Owen (London: Bloomsbury, 2013)

The Hennessy Cognac Gold Cup: The definitive history by Stewart Peters (Stroud: Tempus Publishing Ltd, 2006)

The Irish Grand National: The history of Ireland's premier steeplechase by Stewart Peters (Stroud: Tempus Publishing Ltd, 2006)

Aintree: The history of the racecourse by John Pinfold (Surbiton: Medina Publishing Limited, 2016)

Gallant Sport: The authentic history of Liverpool races and the Grand National by John Pinfold (Halifax: Portway Press Limited, 1999)

Good Horses Make Good Jockeys by Richard Pitman (London: Pelham Books, 1976)

Go Down To The Beaten: Tales of the Grand National by Chris Pitt (Newbury: Racing Post Books, 2011)

Churchill at the Gallop: Winston's life in the saddle by Brough Scott (Newbury: Racing Post Books, 2017)

My Life – and Arkle's by Pat Taaffe (London: Stanley Paul & Co. Ltd, 1972)

My Friend Spanish Steps by Michael Tanner (Sleaford: Michael Tanner, 1982)

The Champion Hurdle: From Blaris to Istabraq by Michael Tanner (Edinburgh: Mainstream Publishing, 2002)

The King George VI Steeplechase by Michael Tanner (Sleaford: Michael Tanner, 1984)

The Cheltenham Gold Cup by John Welcome (London: Pelham Books, 1984)

Who Was Who in Irish Racing by Guy St John Williams and Francis P.M. Hyland (Daletta Press, 2002)

Also: *Steeplechasing in America* 1969 and 1970 and relevant *Raceform* and *Chaseform* form books.

Acknowledgements

Many people have helped in all sorts of ways with the production of this book. I would like to thank in particular Valerie Cooper, Wesley Faulkenberry, Revel Guest, Virginia Guest Valentine, Robert Hall, Arthur Moore and Pamela Morton, each of whom was extremely generous with their time, and whose contributions, more than anything, enabled me to piece together L'Escargot's story.

I am also indebted to: Ben Brain, the late Jeffrey Brain, Pamela Carberry, Philip Carberry, Chris Cook, Milo Corbett, Tim Cox and his incomparable library, Mark Cranham, Stephen Cullinane, Rory Delargy, Toby Edwards, Matthew and Hilary Engel, Averil Forrest, Di Haine, Ben Hanbury, Timmy Hyde, Andrew Kavanagh, David Luxton, Peter Maher, Thomas Matthews, Tony Mawson, Peter McLoughlin, Mouse Morris, Val O'Brien, John Pinfold, David Powell, Brough Scott, Francis Shortt, Derek Thompson, Tim Thomson Jones, Ken White, Guy Williams and others.

The professional skills of Charlotte Atyeo and of Matt Thacker and his team are unsurpassed. I consider myself very fortunate to be able to count them as friends. A big thank you to them. Above all, thanks, as ever, to Edi and Molly for accompanying me on the way – and to our dear, imperturbable Scamp, who left us, aged about 130 in cat-years, as the proofs were waiting to be read.

Index

Note: page numbers followed by * or † indicate footnotes on that page.

Abbot of Knowle 31*
Abletai 52
Aintree viii, 8*, 22*, 125, 149, 173–4, 176, 188–9
Aintree Derby 188, 191
Aitcheson, Joe, Jnr 106
Alaska Fort 146
Alper, Henry 72, 111
Amarind 171
Amberwave Chase 138, 138†
American Grand National 79–80, 104–5
Anglo 11*
Anne Duchess of Westminster viii, 25, 73, 75, 90, 140, 151, 186
Aqueduct 27, 102
Arawak 47
Arctic Ranger 71
Argent 183
Arkle viii, 10, 24, 25, 34*, 42*, 52, 68, 117, 123, 134*,140
Arkle Challenge Trophy 67, 72, 94–5
Armytage, Roddy 50
Ascot 93, 116, 122, 134
Ashe, Arthur 204
Ashville 137–8, 141, 146, 163, 174, 203*
Astrometer 31*
Auteuil 183
Ayr 146

Balding, Toby 104
Baldoyle 66, 86, 140
Ballsbridge 11, 13, 36, 139
Ballydoyle 14, 18
Ballygoran 47, 48, 49
Ballygoran Park 25, 109–10
Ballygowan 4, 10*
Ballykisteen Stud 17
Ballysax 29, 32, 36, 38–9, 50, 66, 84–5, 120, 127, 130, 146, 157, 183–4, 205, 206
Ballywilliam Boy 94
Barbour, Frank 18, 19, 23
Barker, Sean 84, 87, 88, 186*
Barry, Ron 162
Batchelor, Mick 154–5
Battleship x, 2, 34, 105, 197
Bay Tarquin 87
Beasley, Bobby 119, 157–8, 170, 171
Beggar's Way 148
Belmont Park 33, 77, 78, 79, 80, 102, 183
Belmont Stakes 27, 77
Bengough, Piers 178, 179–80
Berry, Frank 141–2
Bicester, Lord 46
Biddlecombe, Terry 53, 55–6, 86, 131, 145, 161, 171, 197
Big Valley 104, 106
Bighorn 131, 132, 133, 142, 153
Billy Barton 20–1, 23, 127*
Black Justice 71

Black Mac 207
Black Secret 126, 143, 150
Blackrath 6–7, 10, 11
Blackshaw, Martin 199
Boat Man 69, 71, 86
Bobby Moore 71
Bobbyjo 205*
Bourke, Jimmy 150
Boyne Handicap Chase 86
Brain, Ben 64
Brain, Jeffrey 64
Broadhead, William Smithson 105
Brogan, Barry 3–4, 9–10, 26, 71–2,
    123–4, 135–6, 142, 143, 199, 200
Brogan, Betty 9–11, 14, 92
Brogan, Jimmy 1–4, 8, 9, 10, 31
Brown Lad 187, 192
Buckingham, John 69, 71
Bula 94, 124, 141, 157, 186
Butcher, Terry 68

Cannonade 182
Captain Christy 157–8, 170, 181,
    183, 185, 186
Carberry, Pamela 54, 83, 205
Carberry, Paul 205*
Carberry, Philip 53, 54
Carberry, Thomas 53
Carberry, Tommy x, 28, 53–4, 55,
    57, 59, 65, 67, 72, 73–4, 75–6, 79,
    81, 83, 85–6, 87, 88, 91, 96, 106,
    108, 112, 114, 118, 123, 125, 126,
    131, 133, 138, 139, 141, 142, 143,
    144, 145, 146, 147–9, 150, 152,
    154–5, 159, 160–4, 165, 167, 170,
    174, 176–9, 183, 185, 186, 187,
    192, 195–202, 204, 207
Carling Black Label Novice Hurdle
    59–60
Carling Black Label Stakes 47

Caro Bello 111
Carolina Cup 99, 107
Cartwright, David 133
Casey, William 17
Castleruddery 168
Cathcart Challenge Cup 73, 97,
    160–1, 170–2, 173, 185–6
Champion Hurdle 53, 58, 68, 72, 94,
    121*, 168
Champion Stakes 63
Charles Dickens 178–9
Charlie Potheen 161–2
Cheltenham Gold Cup vii, viii, 18,
    31, 34*, 88–9, 90–7, 121–3, 124*,
    130,141–6, 158–9, 161–2, 170,
    186, 198
Christmas Handicap Chase 86, 112
Churchill, Randolph 23–4
Churchill, Winston 23–4
Churchill Downs 182
Claiborne Farm 45*, 110*
Clever Scot 138, 140, 161, 172
Clusium 4, 26
Cnoc Dubh 73, 112, 119–20, 125,
    127, 128, 203*
Cobham, Viscount 98–9
Colebridge 136, 181
Colliers Chase 75–6
Collierstown 55
Colonial Cup ix, 98–108, 113, 124,
    133, 138, 147, 152
Comedy Of Errors 157, 168
Connolly, Michael 45
Cook, John 126, 127, 128, 132, 194
Cooltrim Plate 46
Coonan, Bobby 74, 114, 123
Cooper, John E. 78–9, 81
Cooper, Tom 11–14, 18, 25, 34, 45
Cooper, Valerie 13, 27, 45
Cottage Rake 46–7, 123

Courage, Edward 87, 88, 93, 128, 136, 153, 190, 193–4, 199
Crisp 104, 106, 124, 141, 160, 162, 190
Crotanstown Handicap Stakes 103
Culla Hill 148, 149
Cullinan, Tommy 127*
Cundell, Ken 50
Curator 80
The Curragh 27, 29, 38–40, 46, 47, 48, 49, 53, 63, 92, 102, 111, 157
Curtin, T.G. 59 †
Cutlass 183

Daily Express Triumph Hurdle 95, 171
Davies, Bill 8*, 166, 169, 173–4, 175–6, 188–9, 191, 192, 193, 194
Davies, Colin 69, 72
Dewhurst Stakes 49
Dim Wit 127, 128, 142, 159
Don Sancho 127
Donaghmore Handicap Chase 130, 151
Doonbeg 7†
Doyle, L. 10
Dreaper, Jim 122, 126, 138, 140, 151, 152, 169–70, 183, 186
Dreaper, Tom 10, 42, 46, 51, 70, 73, 83–4, 94–5, 97, 121–2, 136
Drumikill 71–2
Drumroan 192*
Dublin Horse Show 27
Duchess Of Pedulas 6
Dundalk 6
Dundrum Chase 66
duPont Scott, Marion 100–1, 105, 147, 172, 186, 197
Durant, Tim 59

Early Mist 11*, 18
East Bound 83–4, 87, 88, 94–5, 152
Easter Hero 19–20, 123
Ebony King 45, 57–8, 71
Elizabeth II: 61
Elizabeth, Queen Mother 98–9, 124, 169
Enda's Choice 91
Ennis, F. 59†
Ennis, Mick 40, 127, 159, 185, 206
Ennis, Peter 87
Epsom Derby x, 13, 24
Ermitage 104
Esban 7†, 139–40, 141, 146, 150*
Escargot 78
Escart III: 7, 119*, 139, 158, 175
Even Keel 116, 134, 135

Fair Vulgan 145–6, 150
Fairyhouse x, 4, 24, 29, 32–3, 35, 45–6, 57, 65, 73, 90, 110–12, 126, 130, 138, 165, 180–1, 192
Faulkenberry, Wesley 100, 107–8
Feel Free 196
Feilden, Randle 186
Final Move 87
Finnegan, Cathal 57
Firm Favourite 65, 66, 70–1
First Of The Dandies 2, 31
Fletcher, Brian 56, 173, 178, 179, 180, 185–6, 193, 198, 199, 200, 201
Flitgrove 8*
Flood, Francis 116, 118
Flying Wild 24–5, 28, 34, 54, 203*
Flyingbolt 10
Foinavon 7*, 11*, 28, 69*, 197
Fort Leney 54–5, 84, 93, 170
Fortina 31
Fortina's Dream 83

Foxrock 115, 140, 168
Foxrock Cup 138–9
Freddie 10*
Free Handicap Chase 183
Free Handicap Hurdle 184
Free Romance 79, 80
Freebooter 33
French Alliance 139
French Excuse 65
French Tan 51, 54–5, 56–7, 67, 86, 93, 95, 96, 97, 102, 106–7, 113–14, 117–18, 120, 121
Frou Frou 144, 174

Gainsborough Chase 117, 169
Gala Day 52
Gale Force X: 34
Gallagher, Redmond 109
Galway Hurdle 54
Galway Plate 3
Garoupe 7†, 162
Garrynagree viii, 42–4, 46, 67, 72, 73, 85, 97, 141
Gay Trip 7*, 55, 80, 93, 131, 142, 145
General Symons 7†
George, Charlie 129
Gibbons, John 168
Gifford, Josh 87, 88
Gillett, Francis Warrington 34
Gilliamstown 1, 3–4, 8, 9, 11, 42, 72
Glanford Brigg 198, 199–200, 201
Glencaraig Lady 76*, 94, 116–17, 118, 122–3, 125, 134, 135, 136, 141, 142
Glenkiln 150
Gloucestershire Hurdle 8, 54–5, 56–7, 66, 94
Golden Miller vii, 31, 123, 124–5, 144, 164, 180

Golden Scene 52
Golden View II: 32
Gowran Park 58, 120, 159
Grand Critérium 49
Grand National vii, x, 2, 6, 9–10, 18–25, 28, 31, 33–4, 56, 73–4, 80, 104*,125–6, 143–5, 154*, 158–9, 162–5, 168, 169, 171*, 172, 174–9, 180, 189–202, 204, 208
Grand Steeple-Chase de Paris 100,183
Grattan Cup 42–4
Gray, David 17
Great Lark 58–9, 203*
Great Noise 88
Greek Vulgan 11
Greenogue 136, 170
Grey Sombrero 131, 132
Grisar, Alfred 19, 21
Guest, Freddie 15–16, 18–19, 22–4, 138*
Guest, Ivor, 2nd Baron Wimborne 15
Guest, Josiah 15
Guest, Raymond x, 13–14, 15–16, 17–18, 21, 22–8, 40–1, 42–6, 47, 49, 58, 61–3, 65–7, 73, 77–8, 81, 88, 96–7, 108, 109–10, 119, 120, 124, 125, 127*, 137–8, 144, 158–9, 162, 163, 164, 166, 180, 182, 183, 184, 191, 193, 195, 203, 204, 205–6, 207, 208
Guest, Winston Frederick Churchill 15
Guest Valentine, Virginia 40, 56, 63, 195, 203, 205, 209
Guinness Chase 11, 146
Guiscard 192
Gwathmey, James Temple 80
Gyleburn 150

Haine, John 132
Hall, Michael 11
Hall, Robert 11*, 12
Hamlet 31*
Hanbury, Ben 37–8, 40, 42, 43, 44, 45, 49–50
Hancock, Bull 45*, 110*
Happy Home 31
Harty, Eddie 106, 107
Hatton's Grace 46–7
Havago 6, 8, 41, 54, 66
Haydock Park ix, 24, 82–3, 84, 85, 86–7, 122, 152, 154–5, 156
Height O' Fashion 46–7
Hennessy Cognac Gold Cup 93, 130, 131–2, 152, 153, 175
Hermitage Chase 149
Herring Gull 54–5, 92, 96, 102, 106, 112, 128
Hethersett 13
High Ken 170, 199–200
High Patches 80, 104
Highland Wedding 73–4, 93*, 107, 180†
Highlandie 59
Highway View 151, 181, 185
Hill, William 44–5
Hobbs, Bruce 2, 197, 203
Honey End 54*
Housewarmer 31*
Hughes, John 82–3, 156
Hunter's Treasure 111, 112
Hurst Park 19
Hyde, Timmy 74, 95–6

In View 33
Inishmaan 111
Inishowen 192*
Inkslinger 108, 133, 138, 147, 152, 158, 159–61, 165, 170, 183

International Steeplechase 33
Into View 121, 122, 123–4, 169
Irish Cesarewitch 46, 49, 52, 56, 103, 139
Irish Grand National 3, 30, 31, 32–3, 74, 119, 126–8, 138*,144, 165, 180–1, 192
Irish Independent Cup 85
Irish National 45
Irish Oaks 47
Irish Sweeps Hurdle 84, 85, 86, 110–11, 114, 157–8, 168
Irwin, Jonathan 14
Isphahan 59

Jacko 81
Jaunty 106
Jay Trump 10*
Jenney, Martha 158
Jockey Club 191
Jockey Club Rooms 37
John Jameson Cup 26, 46, 75
Jomon 140–1
Jones, Tom 137–8, 140–1, 163
Junior Partner 196

Kavanagh, Andrew viii, 43, 44
Kearns, Paddy 26
Keeneland 14, 45*, 110*
Kelleway, Paul 121, 124
Kempton Park 68, 80, 93, 134–6, 141
Kennedy, Darby 36
Kentucky Derby 27, 182
Kerry National 148–9, 166–7, 206–7
Kiely, Paddy 118–19
Kilburn 73
Kilmore 180†
Kilsallaghan 10, 84
Kilvulgan 169

King Candy 57
King Cutler 56–7
King George VI Chase 93, 134–6, 141, 142, 153, 170
King Vulgan 91, 94, 116, 126
King's Sprite 48, 49, 67, 73, 75, 112, 113, 118–19, 127, 128, 139
Kingwell Hurdle 69
Kinloch Brae viii, 7*, 56, 57, 66, 67, 73, 74, 75, 86, 90, 91–2, 93, 95–7, 102, 120, 121, 125, 141
Koko 18–19, 20, 22–3, 138†
Koko Handicap Chase 80

La Gamberge 48
La Lagune 62
Lake Delaware 81
Lambourn 33, 104, 121, 136, 171, 172
Lanzarote 168
Larbawn 7*, 93–4, 95
Larkspur 13, 24, 25, 44, 109
Latham, Frank 6, 7–8
Laurel Park 63–4
Le Mare, Noel 150, 163, 180, 204
Lean Forward 169–70, 185
Leap Frog 67, 86, 121–3, 134, 138, 139, 141, 142
Lee Bridge 18
Lemass, Seán 27
Lenehan, Jimmy 53
Leopardstown 8, 24, 48, 65, 66–7, 76, 115–20, 136, 138–9, 157
Leopardstown Chase 90–1, 92, 116–18, 138, 139, 159, 169–70, 185
Listowel 148–9, 166–7, 206–7
Lloyds Bank Hurdle 187
Lockyersleigh 7†, 119*, 158, 159
Loewenstein, Alfred 19

Longchamp 7, 27–8, 49, 63
Lord Jim 125–6, 132
Lough Inagh 183, 186
Lucky Edgar 132
Lynch, Jack 61
Lyons Derby ix, 7

McCain, Donald vii, 150, 175, 190, 193
Mackeson Gold Cup 130, 131
Mackinnon, Reg 83
McLernon, Bill 113
McLoughlin, Peter 52, 84, 113, 114, 127, 170
McNair, Robert 98
Macroney 118–19
Martin Molony Champion Novice Hurdle 56, 75
Maryland Hunt Cup 20
Massey Ferguson Gold Cup 24, 54, 93
Matthews, Thomas 1, 4
Mawson, Tony 135, 153–6
Meadow Brook Steeplechase Handicap 78, 80–1
Mellon, Paul 100
Mellor, Stan 141*, 146
Middleburg 80*
Mildmay of Flete 141
Mill House 34*, 52
Miss Hunter 143, 145
Mistigo 47
Molony, Martin 36
Monksfield 184*
Moore, Arthur 24, 29, 31, 32, 36, 38, 39, 44, 48, 49, 55, 64, 66, 71, 72, 74, 75, 83, 103–4, 106, 112, 113, 118–20, 125, 127, 128, 130–1, 136, 139, 143, 146, 160, 164, 169–71, 185, 192*

Moore, Dan x, 2, 13, 24, 27, 29–36, 37–8, 44, 45–6, 47, 48, 51, 52, 53–5, 56, 65–6, 73, 74, 75, 77–8, 79, 81, 83, 85, 86–7, 88, 89, 96, 102–3, 105, 116, 118, 124–5, 126, 129–30, 131, 133, 138–9, 140, 143, 144, 148, 149, 151, 156, 158–9, 160*, 162, 163, 164, 166, 168, 171, 172, 179, 183, 185, 186, 190, 191, 195, 201, 202, 203, 206, 207, 208–9

Moore, Florence 30

Moore, Joan 40, 48*, 79, 92, 95, 205–6, 207, 208

Moore, John 110

Moore, Thomas 30

Morgiana Hurdle 158, 168

Morris, Mouse 167, 185

Morton, Pamela 3, 9, 14

Mould, David 24–5, 140–1

Mr Smarty 56

Mr What 6, 11*, 205

Muir 66–7, 70

Multyfarnham 5, 6–7

Murat, Caroline 26, 61, 193

Murpep 52

Murphy, Paddy 58

Murphy, Stan 52, 87

Naas 49, 52, 86

National Hunt Chase 33, 55, 71

National Hunt Handicap Chase 125, 163

National Stakes 48

Navan viii, 42, 43, 51, 91, 92, 94, 116

Neutron II: 48

Newbury Spring Chase 160

Newmarket 37, 49, 50, 63, 92, 103

Nijinsky 103

Niksu 104

No Other 113, 114

Norfolk, Duke of 61

Norman, Tim 25

Normandy 86

Norwegian Flag 7†, 119, 139*, 175

Oakley, Robin viii, 68–9

Oaks 62

O'Brien, Val 46, 123, 142

O'Brien, Vincent 14, 18, 44–5, 137

O'Connell, Daniel 48

O'Connell, Dick 31–2, 38

October Stakes 102

O'Farrell, Michael 14, 53, 56, 66, 70

O'Grady, Willie 58, 90, 92

O'Hehir, Michael 105, 194, 198, 205–6

Old Fairyhouse 32

Oliver, Ken 71–2, 104

O'Neill, Arthur 6

O'Neill, Barbara 6, 8, 205

Osberstown Hurdle 52

O'Sullevan, Peter 27–8, 177

Our Greenwood 192

Packed Home 28, 203*

Paddock Handicap Chase 85

Paget, Dorothy 30–1

Peach II: 106

Pearl Of Montreal 167, 169, 178

Pendil 141, 160, 161–2, 170

Persian War 68–72, 84, 86, 88, 93, 94, 110–11, 112, 124

Phipps, Henry 15–16

Phipps, Mrs Ogden 106

Phoenix Park house 17, 26, 27, 45, 62

Phoenix Park racecourse 26

Pick Me Up 55–6

Piggott, Lester 48, 49, 61
Pilkington, Bill 4, 10, 26
Pinfold, John 163*, 194*
Pitman, Richard 104, 161, 162
Pitt, Arthur 111
Pitt, Chris 179, 194
Pocahontas 25
Pontage 33
Pontin, Fred 126
Portmarnock 66, 86–7
Powell, Jonathan 193
Power Gold Cup 73, 144, 181*
Powhatan Plantation 17–18
Preakness Stakes 27
Prestbury Park 18–19, 56, 102, 120, 123, 141, 158
Price, Ryan 37, 124*
Princess Camilla 177
Prix de l'Arc de Triomphe 27–8, 63
Prix de Madrid 7
Prix du Bourbonnais 7
Probationers' Stakes 47
Proud Tarquin 83–4, 85, 94, 112, 113–14, 127, 128, 130, 132
Proudstown Park 42
Punchestown 11, 26, 46, 56, 75, 83, 85, 87, 113, 117, 129, 148, 151, 158, 168, 183
PZ Mower Power Chase 90

Quare Times 18
Quita Que 160*

Rathangan Stakes 49
Rathganny 5, 6–7
Rathside Chase 113
Ratoath 138, 151
Razor's Edge 52, 57
Red Alligator 11*, 56
Red Rossa 8*

Red Rum viii, 104†, 146, 162, 164–5, 175, 177, 178–9, 180, 189–90, 194, 195, 199–201, 204
Revelry 31, 32
Reynoldstown 172
Richards, Gordon 93, 175
Right Tack 92
Rimell, Fred 56, 65, 101, 131, 175, 196–7
Robinson, Willie 34*
Roman Holiday 88
Rough House 175, 196–7
Rough Silk 167
Royal Danieli x, 2, 31, 32
Royal Relief 87, 88, 94, 113, 134, 135, 160, 186
Royal Tan 11*, 18, 24
Royal Toss 122, 132, 142, 169
Rural Riot 79

Saccone 88
Sacramento 104
Sadler's Wells 32*
Saggart's Choice 132–3
Salaman, Marshalla 'Taffy' 196
Salmon Spray 7*
San-Feliu 65, 175
Sandown 50, 63, 117, 135, 138, 169
Sandymount Chase 83
Sanger, Mrs Michael 183
Scalp Hurdle 8, 66–7, 69, 70, 90, 119*
Schweppes Hurdle 194
Scottish Grand National 146, 150*
Scout 177, 178
Sea Bird 27–8
Sea Brief 140, 151–2, 159
Secretariat 27*, 77*,184
Seminole 25
Sempervivum 71

INDEX

Sergeant Murphy 180[†]
SGB Chase 134
Shadow Brook 106
Shaun Spadah 19[†]
Sheila's Cottage 2
Shields, Sammy 199
Shortt, Francis 57–8, 91
Sir Ivor 25, 44–5, 47–9, 61, 63–4, 109–10
Sir Tristram 182
Smith, Bill 193–4, 199
Smith, Denys 56
Smithwick, Mikey 30, 104, 108, 133, 147, 159, 171
Smithwick, Paddy 30
Smooth Dealer 120, 125, 126, 171*, 203*
Somaten 80, 81
Soothsayer 108, 147, 172, 186
Southern Quest 181, 199–200, 201, 207
Spanish Steps 70–1, 73, 93, 95, 96, 120, 121, 127, 128, 132, 134–6, 142, 153–6, 161, 162, 164, 175, 178, 190, 193–4, 199
Specify 126, 150
Spittin Image 168
Springdale ix, 99, 100–1, 102, 107
Squires, Dorothy 139–40, 175
Stack, Tommy 177
Stella Negra 62
Stillorgan Maiden Hurdle 119
Stonedale 70–1
Stone's Ginger Wine Chase 54, 135
Straight Fort 73, 74, 94, 113, 160
Straight Vulgan 175
Stuart, Gilbert 26
Sundew 152
Supermaster 71
Svejdar, Lady Honor 54

Sweeney, Tony 117
Sweet Dreams 74

Taaffe, Pat 52*, 70–1, 76, 94, 95–6, 97, 106–7, 112, 113, 157–8
Takvor Pacha 2
Tanner, Michael 71, 136
Teal 2
Team Spirit 7*, 10, 33–4, 180[†], 206
Temple Gwathmey Steeplechase Handicap 80, 100, 104, 147, 171
Ten Up 186
The Dikler 7*, 93, 117, 122, 123–4, 134–6, 141, 142, 161–2, 190, 197, 200–1
The Laird 93–4, 134, 153
The Phoenix 17
The Pilgarlic 8*
The Pooka 164
The Tetrarch 36*
Thompson, Arthur 2
Thorner, Graham 145
Thurles 58, 90, 92, 184
Thyestes Chase 58, 120, 159–60
Ticknock Handicap Hurdle 65
Tied Cottage 33, 184
Tingle Creek 138*, 160, 186
Tipperary Tim 20–1
Titus Oates 93, 95, 96, 117, 121, 134, 135, 136, 142, 169
Tom Rolfe 27
Top Bid 104, 106
Topham, Mirabel 163, 166, 176, 191
Topham Trophy 174, 192, 204
Totalisator Champion Novices' Chase 55, 70, 94, 140
Tower Handicap Hurdle 65
Tralee 47, 48
Trentina 83, 85, 95
Tripacer 54

Triple Crown 27, 77, 184†
Troytown 42*
Turcotte, Ron 27
Turnell, Andy 178
Twigairy 75–6, 83, 126
Two-Mile Champion Chase 70, 94,
    113, 124, 160, 171, 186
Tyros Stakes 47

Uttley, Jimmy 69, 72, 112

Vaguely Noble 63
Van Cutsem, Bernard 50
Veuve 75, 130–1, 136, 141, 144, 146,
    160
Vibrax 167
Vichy Derby ix, 7
Virginius 18, 23, 24, 203*
Vulgan 6–7, 8*, 10, 33, 93, 121*
Vulgan's Prince 45–6

Wakley, Nigel 142–3
Walker, Reggie 32
Walwyn, Fulke 33, 34*, 171, 172*
Wanderlure 79
Washington DC International 63–4
Weld, Charlie 111
Weld, Dermot 45
Well To Do 145
Welsh Grand National 23, 65, 122

Westmeath 4, 6, 8, 205
What A Buck 8*
What A Daisy 6–7, 8
What A Honey 6–7, 8*
What A Myth 93*, 124*
Whitbread Gold Cup 94, 165
White Abbess 46
Whitney, Elizabeth 105–6
William Hill Grand National Trial
    150
Williamson, C.P. 22*
Wills Premier Chase ix, 85, 122, 152
Wincanton 69, 70, 86, 120
Winter, Fred 10*, 104, 121, 141, 152,
    160, 170, 172
Wolverhampton (horse) 8*,174, 193
Wolverhampton (racecourse) 72
Woodbine Chase 76
Woodlawn Vase 27
Woolfe, Raymond 100
Workman 2
Wrenfield Track 99
Wustenchef 106
Wyndburgh 154*

Yenisei 168
Young Ash Leaf 87, 88, 104, 106,
    132–3, 142

Zimulator 196